PRAISE FOR *BY CHANCE ALONE*

"Max Eisen's important, timely memoir reminds us that horror does not happen overnight and that no one is immune to it. Villainizing a people, an ethnic or a religious group, can lead to bloodshed and genocide, as it did during the Holocaust. *By Chance Alone* is a testimony to the human experience of needless, senseless suffering. May we learn from it."   —Marina Nemat, author of *Prisoner of Tehran*

"Such were the overwhelming odds stacked against him, Max Eisen should not have survived. Chance, some good people, and not a little luck all played their part, but his dogged determination to overcome the lethal physical and mental onslaught is truly remarkable. It was a short trip to Auschwitz—a long road to recovery. Be sure that one day you will find me rowing a boat on Ebensee in his honor."
—Stephen D. Smith, Executive Director, USC Shoah Foundation

"Max Eisen reveals, with clarity and honesty, his personal resilience and determination to survive against impossible odds, and to bear witness to the horrors of Auschwitz. His humanity and generosity shine through in this powerful and page-turning memoir as he recounts both the cruelty of the SS guards and the kindness and daily heroism of fellow prisoners in the midst of a system designed for degradation, dehumanization, and ultimately death."
—Barbara J. Falk, PhD, MSL, Canadian Forces College/ Royal Military College of Canada/University of Toronto

"Of the all evils of our evil days the Holocaust is the deepest. There is nothing to place against the scale of its vast cruelty, its bestial embrace of hate and murderousness. But it is the very enormity of the Holocaust, its gargantuan horror and bottomless depredations that challenge our ability to 'take it in,' to pierce the immense shadow of its near unspeakable degradations. We need an entrance guide to this inferno, and it is here in the memoir *By Chance Alone*, by Max Eisen, who endured imprisonment and passage through the Auschwitz inferno as a boy. Mr. Eisen's youth began in the pit of that hell, and his later life has been largely dedicated—through talks, education, and now this book—to bearing witness to the Holocaust, and insisting that it is both fact and warning. Mr. Eisen's is the account of one, and there were the millions who did not, who 'escaped to tell' the tale, so that we can morally refresh our response. *By Chance Alone* is a story of great pathos, and told with directness and simplicity, of the sufferings and grief and fear of one boy in a terrible time and a terrible place. The story of one cannot be the story of all, but it may—I am sure this is Mr. Eisen's hope—be a means of securing an intellectual and emotional purchase on the otherwise overwhelming terrors and evil of the greatest crime of this or any other age."

—Rex Murphy, former host of
CBC Radio's *Cross Country Checkup*

BY CHANCE ALONE

Birkenau at the end of the line. Photo courtesy of Ian Jones.

BY CHANCE ALONE

*A Remarkable True Story of Courage
and Survival at Auschwitz*

Max Eisen

HarperCollins Publishers Ltd

HarperCollins Publishers Ltd
2 Bloor Street East, 20th Floor
Toronto, Ontario, Canada, M4W 1A8

www.harpercollins.ca

Library and Archives Canada Cataloguing in Publication
information is available upon request

Maps designed by Larry Eisen

ISBN 978-1-44344-928-1 (hardcover)
ISBN 978-1-44344-853-6 (original trade paperback)

Printed and bound in the United States of America
RRD 9 8 7 6 5 4 3 2

To my beloved first family, who died in a fury of hate but prepared a map for me to travel by. They live on in my heart forever.

To my dedicated and loving present family. Years ago, I could not have imagined I would live to know them. They are my beloved wife, Ivy; my two sons, Edmund Irving and William Larry; my grand-daughters, Amy Tzipporah and Julie Leah; and all my great-grandchildren. They surround me with love, stability, and great joy.

To the numerous students who have attended my presentations. This book is a reminder to stand on guard against radical ideologies and never be bystanders. Their respect and accolades have been a great inspiration to me.

Contents

Author's Note

In the summer of 2012, after two previous attempts, I began to work on this memoir with the editorial assistance of Dr. Amanda Grzyb, an associate professor of information and media studies at the University of Western Ontario and a scholar of comparative genocide. Together, we recorded hours of interviews, which were then transcribed. When we started to put the transcribed interviews together into a cohesive narrative, however, the story just didn't sound the way I had envisaged. In the spring of 2014, we decided to set the interviews aside and start again from the beginning. The process was painstaking. I handwrote the chapters in pencil on 8 ½ x 11 sheets of paper folded in half, and then my wife, my son, or my granddaughter patiently typed them up on our computer. I gave each typed chapter to Amanda, and she edited them and returned them to me with queries and suggestions for additional revisions. Amanda and I met frequently over the next year, and by April 2015—nearly seventy years after my liberation from Ebensee concentration camp—I had completed a draft manuscript detailing my formative childhood years and my subsequent survival during the dark days of the Holocaust.

The dates and places mentioned in this book are described as I remember them, and any factual errors are inadvertent and my sole responsibility. After a seventy-year lapse, I have written my memories as accurately as possible.

Deportation to Havasalya
August 1942

GERMANY

POLAND
(General Government)

Auschwitz II–Birkenau Krakow
Auschwitz I

CZECHOSLOVAKIA

Brno

Prague

Bratislava

Vienna

AUSTRIA

HUNGARY

Budapest

Debrecen

Nyiregyháza

Szatmár-Némety

Csap

Mármaros-Sziget

Kőrösmező

Raho

Havasalya

Tatar Pass

UKRAINE

Kamenets-Podolsky
(Intended destination:
killing fields of
Kamenets-Podolsky)

Moldava

(Start)

Kassa (Košice)

N E
W S

Deportation from Kassa Brickyard to Auschwitz II–Birkenau
May 1944

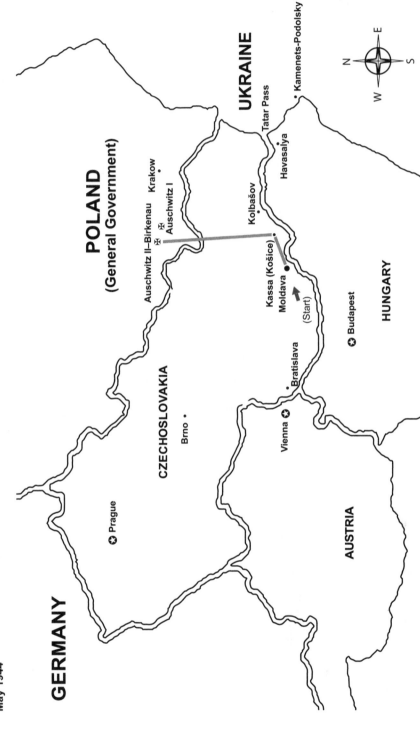

Death March to Ebensee
January–April 1945

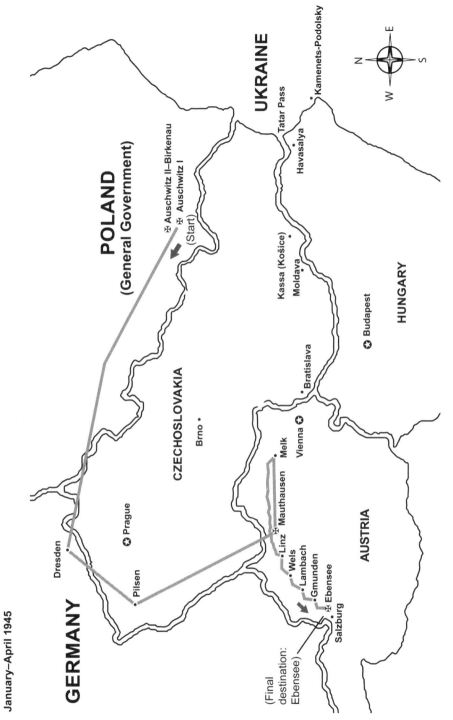

GERMANY

POLAND
(General Government)

☨ Auschwitz II–Birkenau
☨ Auschwitz I
(Start)

UKRAINE

Tatar Pass
Kamenets-Podolsky
Havasalya

CZECHOSLOVAKIA

Dresden
• Pilsen
• Prague ✪

Brno •

Kassa (Košice) •
Moldava •

• Budapest ✪

HUNGARY

• Bratislava

Melk •
Vienna ✪
☨ Mauthausen
• Linz
• Wels
• Lambach
• Gmunden
☨ Ebensee

AUSTRIA

Salzburg

(Final
destination:
Ebensee)

N
E
S
W

After Liberation
May 6, 1945

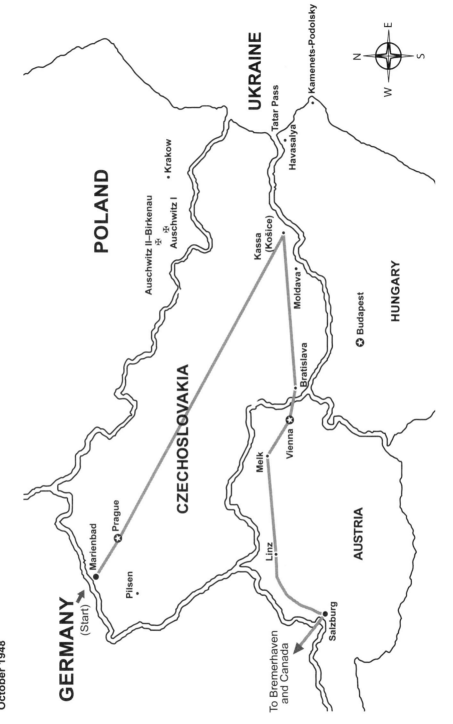

Escaping to the West
October 1948

BY CHANCE ALONE

With my granddaughter Amy for the March of the Living, 1998. This was my first time back at Auschwitz since the war.

Prologue

I n the spring of 1998, I was asked to accompany a group of 150 Toronto teenagers on a trip to Poland, where they would participate in the March of the Living, an annual event that takes place on Yom HaShoah, or Holocaust Remembrance Day. Each year, ten thousand individuals from around the world gather at Auschwitz I and march together to Auschwitz II–Birkenau, where they attend a memorial service for the six million Jewish people murdered by the Nazis and their local collaborators. Amy, my eldest granddaughter, was a part of this group; at sixteen, she was nearly the same age I was when I first entered the camp, in 1944.

As a survivor speaker, I was tasked with filling in the missing pieces: the sounds, the smells, and the feelings of this place. For the first time in fifty-three years, I was going to enter the extermination camp where the Nazis had murdered so many of my family and friends. With no gravesites to visit, this was the closest I could get to their spirits, and I knew it would be a difficult experience for me emotionally.

My arrival at Auschwitz II–Birkenau in May 1944 was a terrifying experience. When I got off the train, I immediately noticed four huge crematoria very close to the platform and nestled among some birch trees. Although I didn't learn their purpose until later, these ominous structures with their massive chimneys were belching flames and smoke, and the brickwork crackled from the heat of continuous use. I recall feeling speechless and short of breath, like something monstrous was going to engulf me. As I lined up on the platform, separated from my mother and siblings, I was helpless and alone, afraid of the unknown. The SS soldiers manning the platform had a brutal look about them, and the skull-and-crossbones symbol on their caps made me panic. When I returned to Auschwitz II–Birkenau in 1998, there were no immediate signs of the towering chimney stacks or the buildings that had once housed the gas chambers and crematoria. The SS destroyed them before they abandoned the camp in January 1945, and the structures now lay in rubble. The birch trees had grown taller, and where once there was mud, there was now green grass cover. Gone was the smell of burning flesh and the skinny prisoners in their flimsy attire, hounded by SS guards. The place looked strangely benign to me now, and I was struck mostly by the sheer vastness of the site, the ruins of the barracks, and the barbed wire. A few kilometres away at Auschwitz I, I saw the barracks where I spent so many nights, the places where I was forced to stand at *appel* for hours, and the spot where the orchestra played. I remembered the hunger, the terror, the constant exhaustion. But I also remembered a few critical moments of advice, small kindnesses, conversations with my fellow prisoners, and the camp hospital that became such an important part of my story.

Speaking in front of the surgery in which I worked at Barrack 21, in 2014.

Sherri Rotstein, one of the organizers of the Canadian contingent of March of the Living, recalled seeing me that afternoon surrounded by the program participants. She said I was staring into the distance and she wondered what I was thinking about. She knew I had journeyed back—emotionally and physically—to a very dark place, but she was heartened by the fact that I was surrounded by Jewish youth, the Jewish future. It was true that being back at the camp filled me with sorrow, but it also gave me comfort as I watched Amy place a picture of my lost family members on the ruins of Crematorium II. I knew they were with us in spirit. And Amy represented the generations of children and grandchildren who'd thrived in the aftermath of the genocide.

My first pilgrimage back to Auschwitz-Birkenau gave me the strength to see, feel, and transmit the horrific deeds that the Nazis had perpetrated there. It was on this trip that I recommitted myself as a Holocaust speaker and educator, work I had first undertaken six years earlier. I have since kept up a rigorous schedule of presenting at schools and other events, and I've travelled back to Auschwitz many times. On one of these trips, my other granddaughter, Julie, joined me. She told me that she remembered hearing the stories of the death camps as a little girl, but it was not until she walked on the grounds of Auschwitz that she really understood the level of the Nazis' deception and the extent of the destruction of human life. She described the impact of seeing my barracks, my bunk, and the places where I laboured. She had always regarded me as a strong, happy, energetic man unscarred by the tragedies that befell my family and me. She told me how much she respected my personal mission to educate as many people as possible about the fate of the Jews during the Holocaust.

4

I made my very first public presentation to a group of grade 13 students at St. Joseph's Catholic high school in Barrie, Ontario, in May 1992. I was nervous and felt myself breathing shallowly as I stood before them and rapidly told my story. I did not have the public-speaking proficiency to transmit my presentation with ease. After I'd finished, I told myself that I'd never do it again. But a few days later, the teacher sent me a thank-you note stating how much the students had appreciated my candour, and how much better they now understood the Holocaust. This feedback gave me the confidence I needed, and I continued to speak by invitation at other venues.

From that day forward, I embarked on a lifelong journey of learning, and I honed my speaking skills for different age groups. Today I speak to grade 5 students and university students, and everything in between. I have travelled the breadth of Canada, from the Maritimes to British Columbia, on speaking engagements, addressing audiences large and small, from classroom size to almost two thousand high school students in a large auditorium.

On one occasion, during a session with an elementary school in Sudbury, Ontario, I was greeted at the door by a group of grade 5 students, and I saw they all wore Star of David stickers on their chests. They asked me if I wanted one too. I put mine on and they escorted me to the classroom, where eighty students were assembled. The teacher informed me that they had read a book entitled *Number the Stars* and were sensitized to the sting of discrimination. I spent two hours with them and told them my story. They had written down several questions on pieces of paper, and I did my best to address them. When we finished, they all lined up and wanted me to sign their question papers and add a comment. Some of them even had extra papers for me to sign for their families. A few months later, a parcel arrived from the school. In it was a felt quilt with twenty panels portraying what the students had learned from my presentation. One panel depicted a locomotive pulling cattle cars. Another showed fishing dories carrying Danish Jews to Sweden. Yet another had an image of my family, including my two brothers holding hands. The quilt was truly a remarkable memorial project, and it reinforced for me the importance of fully engaged learning about history.

Many of the students I speak to are in grade 10, because that's the year when Second World War history is taught. I challenge myself to hold their attention for one and a half hours, as well as through the subsequent question-and-answer period. Often, students approach me after my talks to make comments, take pictures, or ask for my autograph. Teachers and principals have told me many times that they are in awe of how well the students concentrate when I speak. The many letters I receive from the students and their teachers attest to the fact that they really do understand the importance of Holocaust history. It puts their own struggles in perspective, encourages the protection of a democratic society, and helps them speak out when they see injustice.

In addition to speaking at elementary schools and high schools, I have given frequent (sometimes annual) presentations at many universities and colleges, including Lakehead, Trent, Ryerson, Brock, the University of Northern British Columbia, the University of Alberta, the University of Manitoba, the University of Regina, St. Francis Xavier, Western, and Seneca. I've also addressed the York Region police cadets, the Ontario

Provincial Police, and the Canadian Forces College in Toronto. I've made presentations at churches, synagogues, libraries, and community centres during Holocaust Education Week. My out-of-town engagements are very intense; sometimes I make as many as five presentations in three days. These trips can be physically and emotionally exhausting. But I feel they are necessary. And despite the demanding nature of the work, I'm always happy to meet diverse people across our country. If I am available, I will never refuse a request to speak.

While painful, my work as a Holocaust educator has also renewed my spirit. I believe that a new generation can relate to the Holocaust and its lessons with an understanding of how evil can operate when it remains unchecked. It is my hope that the students I meet will combat racism and bigotry wherever they see it, and that they will speak out and make a positive difference in Canadian society. After many visits back to Auschwitz, I can also see that the physical remnants of the Holocaust continue to deteriorate, and that the first-hand witnesses, like me, are moving on in years. I recognize how important it is for survivors to tell their stories, and to honour and remember the people and human potential that was lost. This volume is the final step in my journey as a Holocaust educator, and it stands as my own permanent contribution to this history and to the memory of my loved ones who were lost to this horror.

CHAPTER I

Childhood in Czechoslovakia

W hen I was born in Moldava nad Bodvou, Czechoslovakia, in 1929, my parents could not have foreseen
the danger and destruction that would befall our
family only a decade later.

Our town had a population of approximately five thousand
people, most of whom were Roman Catholic and Reformist
Christian. There were also about ninety Jewish families, totalling
not quite five hundred people. The town had a secure atmosphere
and I had many friends, both Jewish and non-Jewish. At one end
of the main town square there was the Roman Catholic church,
and at the other end there was the Reformist church. Constructed
during the Austro-Hungarian Empire, the baroque-style public
elementary school and the post office were also near the main
square. There was a high school located nearby.

I lived with my immediate family—my father, mother, grandparents, uncle, and aunt—in a large dwelling; each segment of
the family had its own quarters. The businesses of the town were
operated mainly by Jewish owners, including the confectionery

store, a large general store, two bakeries, two pubs, several stores for yard goods and materials, a glazier, and an herbalist. My father owned a pub called the Cellar, where people came to drink and socialize, and where he made and sold a variety of bottled liqueurs in mint, apricot, and chocolate flavours. There was a Jewish butcher and a family-operated bicycle shop that also had a Shell Oil concession to sell gasoline. The town's medical establishment included two Jewish doctors, a Dr. Fried and a Dr. Laszlo, and two Jewish dentists, one of whom, Dr. Gertner, was our family dentist. Two other pubs and a butcher shop were owned and operated by non-Jewish residents. The town's administration was overseen by the equivalent of a mayor, who was also the head of the district of Abaúj-Szántó. There was also a police station in the town.

My mother, my aunt, and my grandmother, like the rest of the town's Jewish women, were intelligent, well-read, capable, and contributing people. They all did volunteer work, such as crafting embellishments for the synagogue and helping the poor. We also opened up the orchards on our property to the needy, who could come and pick fruit in season. When knitted dresses came into style, the women took up knitting as well, making garments for themselves and their daughters.

My extended family included my grandfather, Raphael; my grandmother, Malvina; my aunt Bella; my uncle Eugene, who was my father's brother; and his wife, Irene. While they all shaped my early life, my grandfather taught me many life skills that I still use to this day, and I particularly respected him and valued his attention. My father had another sister who lived in a town called Almás with her husband and children. Their family name was Lazarovits. My mother's helper, Anna, was another

The wedding picture of my Uncle Jeno (Eugene) and wife Irene, taken in 1930.

important person in my early years. Anna came to live with us when I was born, and she was a strong woman in both body and spirit. Although she wasn't Jewish, she knew our customs and could recite some of our blessings for food. In my mind, she was also a part of the family.

I admired my grandfather's strength and knowledge. He'd been a cavalry officer in the Austro-Hungarian Empire and had fought on the Russian front in the First World War. The Jews of Austria–Hungary (who were emancipated in 1867) revered Emperor Franz Joseph, and the elders in my town who were veterans and comrades of that period wore beards and side curls just like his. My grandfather and my uncle Eugene operated the lumberyard on our property. On market day, up to ten farmers parked their horses and buggies in our yard while they sold their goods at the marketplace. I loved horses, so it was a big event for me. Before the farmers left, they would purchase lumber from our yard, and my grandfather recorded the purchases in his big ledger. (After they brought in their harvests, they would pay for their purchases with either grain or livestock.) When they were gone, it was my job, together with my grandfather, to clean up the manure left behind with a broom that had a very long handle. The manure itself was used to fertilize our vegetable garden, and its natural odour didn't bother me. In addition to the steady work of the lumberyard, my grandfather and I also pruned and grafted the fruit trees in our orchard. I always preferred these duties to school, no matter how hard the work.

When my grandfather went to buy sections of forest to be converted into lumber, I was sometimes invited to go along with him. Once, we entered a copse of tall pine trees, and I could hear the wind in the canopy and smell the scent of the pine while my grandfather was checking for the size and girth of the trees to be cut down. In my mind, I wondered if he knew how to get out of the dense forest. But my grandfather showed me how to find the particular signs that would help us navigate our way. On the way out, he taught me about wild mushrooms that were edible and others that were poisonous.

We lived in a rural area where horses and cattle were numerous, and there were occasions when these animals ate grasses that were not good for them to digest, making them bloated and in need of immediate relief. When there was no veterinarian to perform this service, my grandfather was called to release the gas from their bellies. The farmers were grateful that he was available, and his expertise in this area impressed me. I learned many skills by observing him—particularly the importance of a job well done.

My father, on the other hand, had embraced the automobile age in the 1920s and early 1930s, when many social and cultural changes were taking place. At one time, he owned and operated a bus that had a route from our town to Košice,* the capital city of our province, approximately fifty kilometres away. The driver of the bus was also the fare collector, and after a while my father realized that the man was keeping some of the takings and the route was losing money. So within a year, he sold the bus. He also owned a convertible car that he drove for many years, but eventually it became irreparable and was left in the corner of our yard, where it sunk to its axles. My friends and I would sit in the rusted vehicle and pretend to drive it.

---

* This city was known as Košice under Slovakian rule and Kassa when it was governed by Hungary. I have opted to use whatever name the city went by at the time, which means I will sometimes refer to it as the former and sometimes the latter.

My younger brother Eugene (left), Alfred, and me in 1939.

Around 1925, my father established the Cellar, a popular pub where people liked to socialize. I sometimes was given the job of putting exotic labels on the bottles of liqueurs and red wax on the corks, and then adding my father's own seal to the wax. Each bottle was then put into a woven sleeve and dusted with white chalk powder to give it the appearance of age. I sometimes delivered these bottles to customers in the town. I enjoyed my time at the Cellar, and my father allowed me to be his responsible helper. On the cold, dark evenings after Hebrew school in winter, I often went to my father's establishment and waited there until closing time at approximately 8 p.m. He would give me a bit of alcohol to gargle to kill any winter bacteria. I was happy to wait for him rather than going home alone in the dark.

I recall times when my friends and I, after school let out at 4 p.m., bought kaiser buns from Deutch's bakery and then went to the Cellar, where we were allowed to open the spigot on a cask of liqueur and soak our buns under it. All my friends wanted to come to the Cellar to get fortification before Hebrew school. My father, although a strict parent, had a great sense of humour, and it was a happy time for my friends and me.

While my father was the provider, my mother sustained the secure atmosphere and the rhythm of the home environment. She supported our physical and psychological daily needs. I was born in 1929, when she was twenty-five years old and my father was twenty-seven. My brother Eugene was born in 1932, my brother Alfred in 1936. My little sister, Judit, was born in 1943, making a difference of fourteen years between us. All of us were born in the family home and delivered by midwives. My brother Eugene was the smart one, and I felt unfavourable compared to him whenever he finished his homework with little trouble and I did not.

It seemed that he was able to handle the curriculum of both the public school and the Hebrew school easily. There was a natural sibling rivalry between us. Blond-haired, blue-eyed Alfred, on the other hand, was coddled by me and every other member of my family, and was considered the baby until Judit came along seven years later.

* * *

My earliest memory is riding on the crossbar of my father's bicycle as he took me to Hebrew school to introduce me to my teacher. For the first time, I was leaving the security of my family, clutching only a paper bag with a buttered kaiser bun and a tomato for lunch. The school was located next to the synagogue in the centre of town, approximately one kilometre from our home. To a five-year-old boy, it seemed a long distance away. My father handed me over to the teacher, who spoke to me in Yiddish, which I couldn't understand. At home, we spoke Hungarian, my mother tongue.

I was very frightened by this strange new environment. It was a beautiful sunny day and there were many kids my age and older playing games in the schoolyard. Some of them were whittling and making whistles from willow branches. Some had their shoes off and were trying to catch small fish under the rocks of the River Bodvou, which flowed next to the school. Gradually, I made friends and was allowed to walk to school on my own. In the one-room classroom, there were three tables with benches; the children were grouped around them by both age and ability. This was a *cheder* (school) for boys to study the Scriptures (the Hebrew Bible).

A single teacher supervised the entire group, and he was strict and forceful. He used a stick to keep order, meting out punishment against those who did not learn the text properly. I was made to sit on the bench at his right side, and I received punishment regularly for my unresponsiveness. I'm sure that he was trying to demonstrate his expertise as a teacher to my father, who was a respected person in the community. But the more he punished me, the less I wanted to learn.

The pressure of this hostile environment, combined with my classes in the public school system (which I started a year later), was more than I could handle. Not only did I have to learn Yiddish at age five, but I also had to learn Slovak at age six in order to participate in the public school curriculum. Public school ended at 4 p.m., and then we went to Hebrew school until 7 p.m. I also attended Hebrew school on Sundays, and when the Hungarians took over the country in 1938–39, I went to the public school for half a day on Saturdays too. Little time was left for childhood games. My rebellious nature was reflected in my unsatisfactory performance in both schools, which resulted in punishment at home from my father, who expected better results. Luckily, my mother was more understanding, and she came to my rescue on many occasions.

One day, our neighbour Ily's brother arrived for a visit in his fire-red Škoda sports car. I noticed this beautiful car parked in front of their home and was drawn to it like a magnet. In my mind, I saw myself climbing behind the steering wheel and taking off in it. Eventually, everyone came out of the house: Ily carrying a picnic basket; her son, Nori; and her brother, an artist who was tall and smartly dressed. They were going to visit the stalactite caves in Dobsina, approximately one and a half hours away. I was dying to be invited to join them, but when Ily said, "Why don't you come along, Tibor?"—I was known as Tibor when I was young—I was faced with a major decision, because it was our Sabbath and driving in a car was strictly forbidden. If my father found out, the punishment would be dire. Torn between fear and desire, I opted to hop in the car and suffer any consequences later; I was determined not to miss this opportunity.

When we drove through town, I slipped down very low in the car so no one would see me. The stalactites were absolutely amazing, and I had never seen anything like them before. On the way home, my stomach was churning from the fear of what awaited me. It was dusk by the time we arrived. I slipped out of the car, trying not to be noticed, and pretended to be coming home from a long hike. The house was ominously quiet as I approached, and I felt everyone must know of my indiscretion. My father, who must have seen the car return, confronted me as soon as I entered the house and took me out back to the orchard, where he gave me a good whipping. He told me I had committed a great sin by disrespecting the Sabbath. My mother was sympathetic, but she said nothing. I gritted my teeth and took the punishment, but I wasn't deterred from acting on my impulses, then or in the future.

On one occasion, my friend Gaby Lichtman and I ran from the Hebrew school to his house to get some books to read before evening prayers. Every day at Hebrew school, we would break at sundown to pray at the synagogue, then return to school until 7 p.m. This particular day was in the depths of winter, so it was getting dark by five o'clock, which left us only ten minutes before we had to be at the synagogue. I loved books with cowboys and bandits, and I quickly stuffed several under my shirt and winter coat. By the time we got to the synagogue, though, the services were already in progress. I got into line with the rest of the students and said my prayers, but the teacher had seen us arrive late, and he gave me a nasty look. I knew that I was in trouble.

When we sat down, the teacher came over to slap me in the face. I tried to avoid his hand by twisting away because I didn't want to be punished in front of the entire congregation, and when I did, all the books came spilling out of my shirt and onto the synagogue floor. I was hugely embarrassed, and hoped the floor would open up and I could disappear. This incident brought shame to my father, who was also attending prayers, because the entire community had witnessed my poor behaviour. I knew the consequences would be twofold: my father would punish me, and even worse, all the books would be confiscated and I would no longer be permitted to read stories of adventure.

Most of my learning developed outside of the schools, guided largely by my aunt Bella, who read frequently. I learned to read Hungarian sitting on Aunt Bella's lap, and by age five, I could already read books. A beautiful woman, Aunt Bella was an invalid due to polio, which limited her mobility. Despite her disability, she kept a cheerful disposition and took great interest in all our lives. The household routine revolved around her special needs, which were attended to primarily by my grandparents. Grandfather helped her to get up from bed, and Grandmother washed and dressed her, combed her long, silky hair, and braided it and put it up in a bun. Bella was very well read despite a lack of formal education, and she willingly shared her knowledge with us. I enjoyed many moments listening to her repertoire of stories, and my brothers and I vied for her attention.

In addition to Bella's daily routine, the rhythm of our house was also regulated by the seasons. In the summer, when the vegetables were ready for picking, all the women got together for days of food processing. They made preserves, coleslaw, and pickles that would last through to the spring. In the fall, we harvested vegetables such as carrots, radishes, and potatoes, and buried them in sand in our basement cold cellar.

Sauerkraut was a staple food in the home. It was made in the fall in a ritual that I can clearly remember today. We grated enough bushels of cabbage to a fill a large wooden drum, pounded the grated mass with a wooden mallet until it was watery, and then layered the cabbage with bay leaves, corn, choke apples, and peppercorns. When the drum was full, we covered it with a wooden top and placed a heavy stone to weigh it down and initiate the fermentation process.

Making fruit preserves was another annual family ritual. Most of the orchard trees were plums, and we harvested them to make dozens of jars of black plum jam. When the plums were ripe, they were picked and seeded, and the following day, my grandfather and I would set up an outdoor wood fireplace to boil the fruit in a large copper vessel. It took a whole day for the plum jam to cook, so we usually did it during a full moon, which allowed us enough light to work late into the night. When the jam was ready, it was thick and heavy, and my job was to stir the delicious mixture and transfer it into sterile jars. The jars were capped with wax paper and tied with string, labelled by year, and then divided equally among our three families. As a wonderful reward for my hard work, I was allowed to lick any remaining jam out of the copper pot.

Once a week, my mother, grandmother, and aunt would

prepare the dough for the week's bread supply. My job was to transport the dough in a four-wheeled cart to Mr. Deutch, the town baker, on my way to school. After school, I came back to the bakery to pick up the three loaves of bread Mr. Deutch had baked. The bakery was filled with wonderful aromas that delighted the senses. The loaves were stacked on shelves and I searched the name tags for ours. When I got them home, my mother often cut off a big slice for me and coated it with goose fat and paprika.

The three families—my family, my grandparents, and my aunt and uncle—had their own living rooms, bedrooms, and kitchens equipped with wood stoves for cooking and baking. It was wonderful for me because on many days I could choose my menu based on the smells coming out of the three kitchens. I loved fish, and every Thursday in the summers, a local fisherman would bring us two trout, which my mother would bake in butter for dinner. It was delicious. But I detested her tomato soup with rice and would run to another kitchen whenever she made it.

Grain-fed chickens and ducks roamed everywhere in our yard. Geese were fed with boiled corn and kept in their own separate area, where they quickly fattened up. This poultry provided for all our needs, and we were self-sufficient in meats and fats for cooking and baking. The winter diet relied more on meat and fat. Since we were a traditional orthodox Jewish family, we had to process the meat ourselves and render the fat from the geese so nothing was wasted. We ate delicacies such as goose liver, goose rinds with mashed potatoes and sautéed onions, and many other specialties. Feathers and down were plucked and used for pillows and duvets.

A tall fence enclosing our compound had a main gate for vehicles and a small gate for foot traffic. It was patrolled by our three dogs: a large Alsatian named Farkas (*wolf* in Hungarian), and two fox terriers, Ali and Prince. Farkas was the alpha dog, and he was particularly attuned to his surroundings. We could tell by the tone of his bark whether someone approaching the compound was friend or foe, and we always felt well protected.

Because our spacious property lent itself to all kinds of fun, my friends would often gather there to play games such as cowboys and bandits. We would hide in the attic of the old stable or climb the branches of the walnut trees or disappear into the woodshed. We also got into a lot of trouble, for which I often paid the price. When I was eleven years old, I took note of Grandfather's hiding place atop the wardrobe cupboard in his bedroom. This was where he kept special things away from prying eyes. The tall cupboard was half of a his-and-hers set made of ornately carved dark wood. I knew there were goodies up there and was curious to see what treasures I might find. One day, I climbed up on a chair to get to the top, and there I found a bulky leather holster that I picked up in my hands. It was heavy and I wondered if it had a pistol inside. I opened the leather flap, and lo and behold there was a small polished Beretta with a black handgrip. Excited beyond expectation, I was determined to get to town immediately to show it off to my friends. Nobody would be able to top me! I held the holster under my armpit tightly and headed out, all the while hoping Grandfather would not notice it was gone.

When I reached town, my friends gathered around me and I showed them the gun. They were very impressed, and some ran off to get more friends. Soon, I was surrounded by fifteen excited boys, every one of whom wanted to handle the pistol.

Some of them dared me to fire it. I pulled the trigger but nothing happened, so I pulled harder and harder. They began to tease me, saying the gun was a fake. I was angry that it wouldn't fire, and I managed to remove the magazine. We were all amazed to find twelve bullets inside. Fortunately, nobody knew about (or accidentally released) the safety catch. By this time, I was getting very anxious that I would be discovered, so I called an end to the fun and headed home.

I sneaked back into Grandfather's bedroom and replaced the pistol, hoping he wouldn't notice. For weeks after, the boys were still chattering about the gun, but somehow I was never called to account for my actions. In hindsight, I realize how dangerous it was to have a loaded gun and fifteen naive boys grabbing and handling it. If the gun had discharged and injured anyone, there would have been serious consequences for my family, since civilians were strictly prohibited from keeping handguns under Hungarian rule.

On another occasion, eight or ten friends and I were trying to emulate the habits of older boys in the town who were doing more "grown-up" things. Smoking was forbidden, but at eight years of age, we did not take that as a deterrent. We had no money, so I volunteered to get some from my father's till at the Cellar. I went to the store and told the shopkeeper that the schoolteacher had asked me to pick up cigarettes. I put the money on the counter and was given ten cigarettes wrapped in newspaper. My friends and I took off to a nearby secluded mountain area to light up. Everyone was inhaling and blowing smoke rings, and soon we all became dizzy. We were coughing and spitting, and it was not a pleasurable experience for any of us, but we wanted to be like the older boys.

When I returned home, my mother immediately smelled smoke on my breath and knew exactly what I'd been up to. She told me in no uncertain terms never to do it again. In spite of the warning, I continued to smoke with my friends whenever we managed to scrape together some loose change.

Dr. Fried, our family doctor, was an elegant man who always smoked a cigar when going on his walks about town. I found the cigar smoke very pleasing and would follow him around to get a whiff as he walked. Eventually, my friends and I decided to pool our money to buy one large Cuban cigar to share. We returned to my family's property with the treasured purchase and stole away inside the large chicken coop. We tried to light the cigar, but we didn't realize that we had to clip the end to create an airway for the smoke. Everyone tried unsuccessfully to light it, progressively chewing up more and more of the end, making a mess of it. As matches from all the lighting attempts accumulated on the floor, the straw started to smoulder and soon smoke filled the small pen. It attracted my grandfather, who opened the door and yelled, "Get out! You are burning down the chicken coop!" When we got outside, I could see smoke coming from every crevice. My friends took off, leaving me to face the talking-to from my grandfather. But still we were not deterred. We started making corncob pipes and smoking dried leaves instead of tobacco. It was awful stuff, but we kept at it during the fall, when there were plenty of leaves to use. I carried on smoking until I was twelve, when I had to leave home for my apprenticeship.

Looking back, I see how outrageous some of my actions were. I also see how much thought, effort, and work went into running the household, and how much I took for granted. My mother fed us a nutritious, balanced diet, cooked from scratch every day, and she gave me a spoonful of fish oil with a drop of syrup for additional health before I left the house for school. She was also an amazing seamstress, and she made many of our clothes at home. How she managed with no running water, no washing machine, and no other modern conveniences is beyond my comprehension. She must have experienced stress and tension in the course of her day's work, and I realize now how much she sacrificed for her family's well-being.

Chapter 2

Summers on the Farm

My mother's family lived approximately two hundred kilometres away in a small farming community called Kolbašov, near the large city of Michalovce. Grandmother Friedman and my two unmarried uncles, Herman and Pavel, ran the large family farm, where they produced corn, grain, and flax. They had a herd of milk cows, sheep, and goats, as well as several teams of horses that they used for tilling, hauling, and other kinds of work. This was a very enterprising farm with many young people hired to help out. At sunrise the cattle were taken out to the various pastures to graze, and they were brought back at noon and again in the evening to be milked by hand into pails. The farmhands processed the milk in separators for skimmed milk and butter. They made cheeses from sheep and goat milk. At the end of the day, the teams of horses were also returned from the fields, unharnessed, groomed, and freed to take a run to the water trough.

My first extended visit to the farm was in 1935, when I was six years old. I spent the entire summer there that year, almost two months. I returned again in the summers of 1936, 1937, and 1938. Summer holidays at the farm were a time of freedom, with no public school or Hebrew school. I felt so unconstrained. Many of my cousins from nearby towns came for the summers as well, and we were a happy group of eight or ten children. I was particularly attached to two older cousins, Edith and Lily Burger. Another cousin, Laly Friedman, was allowed to saddle his horse and ride at any time, whereas I could ride only in front of my uncle on his saddle.

We children had so much to occupy our minds. We used to visit the newborn calves, putting our hands in their mouths and letting them suck our fingers with their toothless gums. We picked wild strawberries in the fields. Uncle Herman and Uncle Pavel were very busy running the farm, but they always managed to find some time for us. We were given the task of taking the sheep and goats to pasture. Trying to keep them all together was a challenge, especially when the goats wandered off, climbing ever higher on the hillside. I loved it when my uncles took me on their saddles and galloped off to faraway fields to see how the harvesting work was progressing.

At the end of each long day of activities, we children were dirty and dead tired, and we were allowed to go to a nearby mountain stream to splash around and wash. The water was freezing cold.

The first summer, I met a local boy my age, and every year we spent time together exploring the wider area. One day we found a cemetery that was overgrown by trees, and he told me there were ghosts there that came out every night. I was scared, but we dared each other to go inside. Neither of us was able to muster enough courage alone, so we went in together. In the middle of the cemetery, there was a large pear tree loaded with huge fruit. We could not reach them, so we found some stones and pelted the branches to shake a few loose. The pears were sweet and juicy, and I really enjoyed them. We had all kinds of fruit in our orchards at home, but the fruit from someone else's garden always tasted better. We revisited this cemetery quite often.

My last trip to the farm was in the summer of 1938, when I was nine years old. My visit was interrupted midsummer when my uncle Herman abruptly took me to the railway station and sent me back home. Czechoslovakia was under threat of invasion by Nazi Germany and the situation had become unstable. I never saw my mother's family again. At nine, I didn't fully understand what was taking place, but I noticed the rising tensions in my hometown. Since we lived so near to Hungary, the streets had to be patrolled at night and the Czechoslovakian army was moved up to reinforce the border. As children, we were excited to see the soldiers with all their equipment, and we didn't realize the dangers looming ahead.

CHAPTER 3

Big Changes

Czechoslovakia was established as a democracy under the terms of the Versailles Treaty. Its population was made up of four ethnic groups: the Czechs, the Slovaks, the Hungarians, and the Sudeten Germans. The official languages were Czech and Slovak, but each ethno-regional group spoke its own language (including German or Hungarian in some regions). We lived in the eastern part of the country and spoke Hungarian at home and Slovak at school. We revered Tomáš Garrigue Masaryk, the president of Czechoslovakia from 1919 to 1935. When he died in 1937, an era died with him. In particular, the Jewish people lost a president under whose leadership they'd flourished for seventeen golden years.

Not long after Masaryk's death, civil disobedience erupted in the Sudeten part of the country, which shared a border with Nazi Germany. Hitler capitalized on this civil strife and used it to wrest the Sudetenland away from Czechoslovakia. In 1938, he summoned the leaders of Britain, France, and Italy to the Munich Conference to make the German annexation of the Sudetenland a reality. Our own president, Edvard Beneš, was excluded from the meeting, so the fate of the territory was decided without his input and in contravention of the Versailles Treaty, which said that Great Britain, France, and Italy would come to the aid of Czechoslovakia if its neighbours threatened it. But Hitler had threatened war unless they agreed to allow Germany to annex the region, and so they acquiesced. It was ironic that two democracies, Britain and France, signed away a fellow democratic country to appease a dictator. The country's fate was decided by the stroke of a pen. Not a single bullet was fired during the partition, yet it opened the floodgates to the Second World War.

Upon his arrival back in Britain, Prime Minister Neville Chamberlain waved the agreement he had signed with Hitler and the other leaders and declared it to be a guarantee of "peace for our time." He wrote in his diary that he had no intention of going to war for a faraway country whose name he could not even pronounce. The French did not realize that they had signed away their eastern defences, and there was champagne flowing in Paris to celebrate peace with Nazi Germany. Six months later, on March 15, 1939, German troops crossed the Czechoslovakian border and took control of Prague. Czechoslovakia ceased to exist, and the country was partitioned into three regions: Bohemia and Moravia became the protectorate of the German Reich, overseen by Hitler's deputy Reinhard Heydrich; the fascist autonomous state of Slovakia was created under the leadership of a Roman Catholic priest, Dr. Jozef Tiso; and the eastern part of the country, inhabited by Hungarian-speaking people, was given to Hungary under the fascist leadership of Regent Miklós Horthy. The Czechoslovakian Jewish population was left with a deep sense of dread.

One day in 1938, about ten of my father's friends came to our home to listen to a major speech by Adolf Hitler on my father's crystal radio. All of us understood basic German, and I heard Hitler's poisonous words pouring out of the box. At one point he said, "*Wir werden die Juden ausradieren*" (We are going to eradicate all the Jews of Europe). My father and his friends appeared shocked by this statement, and I felt in my gut that something terrible was going to happen.

Indeed, life as we knew it was about to change in ways we could not have imagined. In March 1939, when I was ten, the Slovak bureaucracy in our town was dismantled and the Hungarian fascists took over. We were taught to sing the Hungarian national anthem in readiness for the new regime. There was no school to attend because the Slovakian teachers had left, and the people of the town prepared to greet the new authority by erecting a large victory gate with a sign that read "Welcome, our Hungarian liberators." The flag of Hungary and ribbons of red, white, and green were displayed throughout the streets and on homes. We Jews could not foresee what these changes meant for us, and as a child, I was unaware of the deeper dangers until some days after the Hungarian troops arrived, bringing with them an overt ideology of anti-Semitism.

For Jews like us, allegiance to this new regime meant that we had to succumb to a fascist ideology that was alien and unfriendly. Yet we had to find ways to ingratiate ourselves to this change. My grandfather, for example, took me up to the attic, where he stored his old officer's cavalry uniform from the days of the Austro-Hungarian Empire. We cleaned the clothes, brushed and polished the boots, and attached all his medals. He presented quite a figure to me in this uniform. All Jewish veterans who'd fought in the First World War on the side of the Austro-Hungarian Empire gathered in their uniforms in front of the welcoming gate to show their old Hungarian stance. I was too young at the time to understand the significance of what was going on. I saw the Jewish adults in our town trying to adapt themselves to the new reality, but they hid their deepest fears as they suddenly found themselves thrust into a hostile fascist system, knowing their vulnerability as Jews.

After several hours of waiting in the centre of town, we received word of the arrival of the Hungarian troops. In the distance, we observed a column of soldiers, led by an officer on his horse, slowly marching toward us. I looked at the soldiers as they passed and was not impressed by their appearance. Their uniforms were dirty and full of patches—no comparison to the Czechoslovakian army, which was always so well outfitted. A cry went up from the crowd, and everyone sang the Hungarian anthem as the military column marched into the town square. There, the welcoming committee officially handed over our town from Czechoslovakia to the new Hungarian administration. The ceremony ended, and the soldiers were dismissed and allowed to wander throughout the town. They headed to the pubs, where townspeople gave them food and other provisions. My father's establishment, the Cellar, had a big sign that read "Free drinks to our liberators." In a span of approximately two days, my father's inventory was exhausted and he could not afford to continue with this largesse.

Hungarian soldiers were posted as guards on several roads coming into the town as if we lived in a war zone. I experienced my first encounter with Jew-hatred under Hungarian rule when I crossed into town over the railway tracks and was stopped by a guard who recognized my cap as Jewish. He yelled at me, "You dirty Jew, where are you going? You should take off your cap when you see me!" When I told my father of this encounter, he prepared little bottles of schnapps for me to give to guards as I entered their posts, which allowed me to reach my destinations unharassed from that point forward.

With the new administration, our town was suddenly flooded by shoppers from Hungary. They came on bicycles, by horse and buggy, or on foot to buy yard goods, hardware, shoes, and anything else that they had not seen in a long period of time. I felt overwhelmed by all these strangers buying up everything they could find. Soon after, the gendarmes (police) arrived, along with new teachers and bureaucrats, and our town became the seat of the province of Abaúj-Szántó. The new currency was the Hungarian *pengö*, which replaced the Czech *corona*.

School started and we met our new Hungarian teachers. They taught us in Hungarian, and Slovak was no longer officially spoken in our region. Jewish businesses and stores operated as best they could, but the shopkeepers could not replace goods that sold out because the sources were now across the border in the Nazi protectorate. Amid all these changes, we suddenly realized that my mother's family now lived in fascist Slovakia and we were in fascist Hungary. We could communicate by post, but we could not travel across the border, which meant my summer holidays with my grandmother, uncles, and cousins were now only a memory.

With all these changes, we Jews felt ostracized, and ugly Jew-hatred started to surface in many ways: name-calling, fights with other kids, and newspapers filled with propaganda about Jews coming to Hungary from the east (Ukraine). Eastern Jews were depicted as having hooked noses and beards, wearing dirty black garb, and coming in hordes to endanger the lives of local populations. One story, entitled "*Tarnopolbol Indult El*" (He started out from Tarnopol), was meant to convince the Hungarian population that Jews were threats to be wary of. Repeated enough times, lies become a "truth" that people believe. Even I was confused and ashamed by the characterization because it was so oppressive, one-sided, and dehumanizing. I did not want to be singled out in such a negative way. I tried to insulate myself from the horrible, hurtful rhetoric, but it was a constant daily burden.

In hindsight, I see how negative pressures were continually assaulting us in our daily lives, and we had to get accustomed to living with this adversity. The Jewish community tried to maintain hope that this persecution would pass with time, and we came together to make life bearable in spite of the hardships. It was the parents who dealt with many of the new stresses, but at least our family was still intact. It was still only 1939, and we had many unknown and unthinkable obstacles ahead of us. But we could live only one day at a time, and each of those days carried more than its share of hardship.

CHAPTER 4

Life under Hungarian Rule

T he Hungarian bureaucracy was in full control of the town's offices when I started grade 5 in September 1939. All boys were required to wear a navy cap with the Hungarian emblem on it, and to salute any military officers and teachers we met on the street. The new Hungarian teachers were noticeably stricter, especially with Jewish students. I felt additional pressure, not only because I was Jewish but because I had an attention deficit disorder and became easily bored with subjects in which I struggled, such as mathematics and grammar. I liked geography, history, and art, and while I loved music, I could not get the hang of reading music notation.

During teacher changeovers, we often let off steam by throwing crayons, sponges, and other things around the classroom. Of course, this behaviour was always noted and reported by the next teacher. As punishment, we were handed over to the physical education teacher after classes and ordered to do hundreds of leapfrogs and push-ups in the schoolyard. Those of us who could not keep up were beaten with a stick.

My family in 1940: Alfred (left), my mother, me, my father, and Eugene.

In 1940, the government posted more edicts in town spe-
cifically targeting the Jewish community. Jews were no longer
allowed to use radios, and we were ordered to take our crystal
sets to town hall and relinquish them. Without radios, we were
cut off from the outside world and we could receive our news
only from government-censored newspapers. An edict that particularly affected my family barred Jews from selling alcohol and
tobacco. My father lost his main source of income when his business was confiscated without any compensation and all his merchandise was handed over to the authorities, along with the key
to his establishment. Another oppressive edict decreed that all
Jewish families be photographed by the police, and we were certain those photographs were then used as a surveillance tool. At
school, we had weekly cadet drills with a military officer. Jewish
students were always placed at the end of the column and made

to carry shovels and rakes, while non-Jewish students carried wooden guns at the front. Upon arrival at the shooting range, the Jewish students had to clean, rake, and shovel the area while the others performed drills with their wooden guns. Marching through the town, I was acutely aware of being a second-class citizen, and I dreaded this humiliating weekly session at school.

In 1941, all Jewish males from ages eighteen to forty-five, married and single, were sent away to labour battalions. My father, my uncle, and all the others were taken to work in mines, forests, and military installations on the Eastern Front. They had to pack a backpack with winter clothes and boots, and they paid their own fare to their designated postings, leaving their families to fend for themselves. This, of course, was a physical and economic hardship for the entire Jewish community, including my mother, my grandparents, and all the children. Suddenly, my mother was the single parent of three children, and she did her best to meet all the demands on her and hide her worries from us. We children also had to pitch in and do work that was normally done by adults. The whole Jewish community had to support the needs of its members and provide the necessities of life, particularly for destitute families. Our Hebrew classes ended when our teacher was also taken away to the labour battalions.

The men in the labour battalions were not compensated for their work, and they were given only a one-week furlough once a year. When they arrived home for that visit, it was a huge event. And when they had to leave again, it was a very sad goodbye. To send them on their way, every household was busy for days, preparing food and provisions to help sustain the men while they were gone. With my father and uncle away, my grandfather was in charge of the daily grind and morale in my home. The gaping absence of our men particularly struck me during Rosh Hashanah (the Jewish New Year) when there were only old people, women, and children at the synagogue.

Another crucial edict forbade Jewish people from employing non-Jews, which meant that Anna, our household helper, could not be with us anymore. When she refused to leave us, the gendarmes came to remove her forcibly from our home. Anti-Semitism reared its ugly head again when the Jewish population was blamed for the wounded soldiers who came back (some with missing limbs) from the Russian front in late 1941 and early 1942. Jews were held responsible because Hungarians claimed that all the Russian communists were Jewish.

In the spring of 1942, we received word by telegram that all the members of the Friedman family, my mother's relatives, had been deported from Slovakia to an unknown destination. We had no way to communicate with them or find out where they were. My mother was devastated, and I thought of all the time I had spent with them during my summer holidays, especially my two cousins, Edith and Lily, who were close to my age. It was unthinkable that people could simply be removed from their homes and were suddenly gone, disappeared. I could tell from my mother's demeanour that this news weighed heavily on her and filled her with worry. She had no idea what had happened to her own mother, her brothers, or her three sisters and their families.

One day, months after their deportation, we received a post-card that read, "We, the Friedman family, are all here together. We are working on farms and we are awaiting your arrival. (signed) The Friedman family." Other families in our town received similar cards, which were printed with a big German eagle and a stamp that said "General Government Lublin

District," the new name of the German-occupied area of Poland. While the postcards may have provoked suspicion in some members of the community, they gave me a deep sense of relief. I felt hopeful to learn that my relatives were alive months after they had disappeared.

* * *

In August 1942, a few of my friends came to our orchard to pick fruit for their families. As we played and stuffed ourselves with fruit, we challenged each other to see who could climb the highest in a very tall walnut tree. This was a risky activity because you could easily miss a foothold or handhold on a branch and be severely injured.

Suddenly, I heard my dog Farkas barking ferociously. I could tell that some strangers had entered our yard and he was warning us of the intrusion. Then I heard my mother call for me to come back to the house. When I arrived, I saw two gendarmes reading from a document to my grandparents, my mother, and my aunt. I could not imagine the contents of the document, but from the looks on their faces, I understood it was a serious situation. It was an order that my mother, my aunt Irene, my two brothers, and I each pack a bundle and prepare to be removed from our home. My grandfather and grandmother were excluded from this directive, as was Aunt Bella. My grandfather pleaded with the gendarmes, saying that my mother and aunt were Hungarian citizens, and that our family had lived in the region for many generations. The gendarmes said that they were simply following orders. My grandmother helped to pack food while my mother gathered other necessities for our departure. When the gendarmes were distracted, my grandfather slipped my mother and Aunt Irene a handful of money. The gendarmes then walked us out of our yard; my dog Farkas had to be restrained by my grandfather.

I was thirteen years old, Eugene was ten, and Alfred was six. We were now a group of five travelling into the unknown, and we felt frightened and powerless. My father and Uncle Eugene were still at the labour battalion in southern Hungary, hundreds of kilometres away, and they didn't have any idea that this was happening. The gendarmes took us to the railway station, where some fifteen other families were being held with their bundles; there were approximately eighty people in total. We were eventually loaded into an open cattle car with two gendarmes who sat with their feet dangling over the edge. We were jostled about in the car and tried to make ourselves somewhat comfortable. We had no idea where we were going or how long the journey would take.

The first stop was the city of Kassa, about sixty kilometres away. There, our cattle car was attached to another transport that already had several cars loaded with people. We travelled on, eventually arriving at a station called Szatmár-Némety in Transylvania. Some minutes after our arrival, several local Jewish men and women appeared to distribute fruit, bread, and water to us. This was a wonderful gesture on their part as we were in great need of food, and I wondered how they had learned of our plight. We remained in the car at this station all night. We had only two buckets to use as toilets, and when they were full, someone got off the train and emptied them. Being in close quarters with so many others was beginning to wear us down, and the sleep deprivation and other irritations began to show.

The next day we travelled in a northeastern direction along the Tisza River, toward the Karpathian Mountains. At this point, after three days in the open car, the nights were feeling quite chilly. The older people were full of groans and aches and pains, and we all missed our home comforts and freedom of movement. We reached the next stop, a place called Máramaros-Sziget, in the middle of the night. Our transport was shunted to a siding, where we stood the whole of the next day without movement. I began to wonder anxiously if it would be better to get where we were going or stay where we were.

That evening the train started up again, and we realized it was going back in the opposite direction. Eventually, we arrived again at Szatmár-Némety, and miraculously the Jewish citizens supplied us, again, with food and water. It was hard for us to understand the manoeuvring of our captors. We hoped that we might be returning home, and we were very disappointed when the train moved once more to Máramaros-Sziget. This time, the track beside us had a military hospital train loaded with injured Hungarian soldiers coming from the Russian front. I recall one heavily bandaged officer who hatefully yelled out to us in Hungarian, "You stinking Jews, you will be swimming in the Dniester River like fallen leaves." His outburst was frightening and strange to me.

The train continued its journey along the Tisza River beside the Karpathian Mountains and eventually arrived at a town called Raho. By now, we had been travelling for nearly six days, and we were eager to get out of the boxcar. The train continued on to a small station called Kőrösmező. This was the end of the line for us, and we were finally able to gather our bundles and leave the boxcar.

There were eight hundred to a thousand of us milling about, and Hungarian military police officers soon took charge. They ordered us to start climbing a steep, rocky road. With great difficulty, we arrived at a mountain plateau that had several large sheds and a sawmill where lumber was being processed. This place was called Havasalya, and it was located near the Tatar Pass, which led to Ukraine. The police moved us to an area of long tables, and we were processed and asked for identification. Our bundles were checked for hidden valuables and currency. They checked all our belongings thoroughly, even looking at the shoulder pads in our jackets and inside loaves of bread. One family was beaten for hiding a gold watch on a chain and several rings; these items were discovered when a policeman dipped his bayonet into a jar of jam and pulled out the hidden valuables.

My mother had charged me with hiding our currency during the journey, and I had placed it inside the lining of my boots. When I saw the police so thoroughly checking every person, I told my mother that I was afraid I would be caught. She told me to act normally, but she looked worried. When it was our turn to be inspected, the officer requested our documents and then asked us where our men were. My mother and aunt told the officer that they were in the labour battalions, and he simply said, "Move on." I breathed a big sigh of relief.

Once the entire group was processed, we were directed to three sheds, where we bedded down with approximately three hundred people per shed. The sawdust on the floor cushioned us somewhat as we slept, so it was more comfortable than the cattle car. But the shed was very hot during the day, and its gappy lumber walls made it cold and drafty at night. We staked out a spot for our family, and this became our home for the next two weeks. There was no water available at the site and we had to fetch it in pails from quite a distance away, guarded all the while by gendarmes. The Tisza River came from the mountains, and it was clear and ice cold. We used this water for drinking only— there was never enough left to bathe in or wash our clothes. Our food rations consisted of a bowl of soup a day; those who had money could buy a loaf of round black rye, the size of a kaiser bun, from the local Ruthenians who came to the area where we filled our pails. Now the money that I had hidden was a blessing, and it was able to sustain us and others who were needy in the weeks that we were there. We paid dearly for this bread and the exchange had to take place clandestinely, when the guards were out of sight.

Families who went before us had written their names on the wooden planks that formed the wall of the shed. Each person's family name was written down, along with the day of their departure and the name of their destination—Kamenets-Podolsky. Thousands of names from previous transports were scribbled on the walls. Each one was like a life marker, a statement to remind the world that these people had lived.*

At the end of the second week, we were all assembled and the captain in charge, a moustached Hungarian officer riding on a big horse, told us that the next day we would be taken in trucks to our workplace at Kamenets-Podolsky, and that we should be in front of our shed with our bundles early the next morning. We wrote our names on the walls, just as the others before us

---

* In August of 1941, twenty-three thousand mostly Hungarian Jews were murderd by the Nazi Einsatzgruppen, the first mass murder of Jews by the Nazis in World War II.

had, and my mother lightened the load by removing from our belongings anything that was not useful.

The next morning, we were loaded onto a convoy of trucks under the supervision of the Kommandant. He wished us a good journey and gave the order for the trucks to move out. It was a Saturday morning, and the trucks laboured to climb to a higher elevation until we reached the Tatar Pass. From there, the road gradually descended. We were now in German-occupied Ukraine.

All at once, someone in my truck yelled that the Kommandant was approaching from behind at full gallop. When he reached us, he ordered our driver to stop, then repeated the process until he caught up with the lead truck. He then announced that we were not going to Kamenets-Podolsky after all and instead were going home. I wasn't sure that I'd heard him right and it took a while for this reality to sink in. There was a big cheer from all of us and I began to think happily about my home, my grandparents, my dogs, and getting back to a normal life.

The Kommandant told us to get off the trucks with our bundles, walk back to the sawmill, and then continue down the mountain to the railway station at Kőrösmező, where a train was waiting for us. He told us that we would have to buy our own tickets for the journey, and that those who had money would have to pay for those who did not. After we had bought tickets for others, my family was left with very little money. But we were a happy bunch, and the way forward was a fast downhill run to the train.

Our group of about eight hundred people occupied the entire train. This time, we were not in a boxcar and sat in seats like normal people. We were a dirty, smelly bunch and there wasn't a clean garment among us, but we were happy. At the first stop, we had time to wash our hands and faces with some soap that my mother had managed to buy. Halfway through our three-day journey home, she decided that we would get off in a town called Csap, where we had relatives. My mother did not want us to arrive home looking and smelling as we did. We said goodbye to our friends on the train and walked to our relatives' home. They were shocked to see our condition and hear the story of our horrific journey. They gave us fresh, clean clothes and a good meal, and it felt wonderful to sleep on a clean straw mattress on the floor.

My mother sent a telegram to my grandfather saying that we were on our way back home and telling him our approximate arrival time. The next day, we said our thanks and goodbyes to our relatives and walked to the station to get on the train. The ride home seemed to take forever, and the hours felt like days. I passed the time thinking about the stories I would tell my friends about our adventures over the past three weeks. I also thought about the importance of family and home, and I vowed not to complain again about trivial things.

When the train stopped in our town, we gathered our belongings, got off, and started to walk toward our home. As we came around a bend in the road I could see our house, the most beautiful sight. As we got closer, Farkas came flying through the gate at full speed. When he reached us, he stopped abruptly, stood on his hind legs, and licked me all over my face. He greeted each of us in turn and truly had an amazing heart.

My grandfather and grandmother were waiting for us in the yard, and we were so happy to see them again. They had tears in their eyes and they hugged us all. I ran to say hello to Aunt

Bella in her quarters, and it was a very emotional reunion for everyone. There was a wonderful aroma of chicken paprikash cooking on the stove, and my grandmother had filled the table with salads prepared specially for our return. We relished this food so much that I could hardly fill my belly. After lunch, I went outside to check out the yard where all the chickens, ducks, and geese were scratching for food. The orchard was bursting with ripening fruits and I hugged every single tree. This was one of the happiest moments of my life.

Many of my friends who had not been deported came over and we went swimming in the Bodvou River. I was very excited to see them, and they were eager to hear the stories of our journey. Several days later, my father and uncle arrived home, and the family was whole again. The day we were deported, my grandfather had sent my father and uncle a telegram explaining our situation. They asked for leave from the labour battalion to come back and try to find us, but their request was denied. Two weeks later, their unit was moved to a new location and they had an opportunity to get away. They came home and discussed with Grandfather where we might have been taken. They went from station to station asking if anyone had seen a transport of Jewish people in cattle cars, and collecting valuable clues as to the direction we might have gone. They arrived in Kőrösmező two days after we'd left for home. Eventually they caught up to the train, only to find out that we'd got off the previous day at Csap. When they backtracked to Csap, we had already left for home. When they finally reached us, we were happily reunited.

Many years later, I learned from a book about the 1942 Hungarian deportations that the government, which had previously ordered the deportation of some forty thousand Jewish people, had debated whether to allow the last group—our transport—to go to its final fate. We were shunted back and forth as the politicians deliberated. They ultimately decided not to proceed with our deportation, and so we were miraculously saved from the jaws of death. I learned later that all forty thousand previous deportees were taken to Kamenets-Podolsky by the Hungarian military police and murdered by the Einsatzgruppen, the Nazis' mobile killing units, on the shores of the Dniester River.

* * *

I had missed the first two weeks of classes and had increasing difficulties adjusting to school discipline. By that point, all Jewish students had to sit in the back of the classroom. We were singled out by both the students and the teachers. My friends and I felt humiliated and ostracized from the rest of our classmates, to whom we had previously been equals. I could not concentrate, and I was still sorting out the events of the previous month in my mind. Eventually, the school advised my mother that I would be removed because of my lack of discipline. I felt ashamed, but I was also happy. This new arrangement gave me time to help her with her various chores around the house, help my grandfather in the lumberyard, and do a lot of reading.

A few weeks into this routine, my mother realized that I was not learning anything productive for my future. She decided to take me by train to Kassa, where her cousins operated a small kosher restaurant. There were quite a few tradespeople who were steady customers at this restaurant. One man had a fur shop, and they asked him if he would take me on as an apprentice. My mother and I went to meet the owner, and I was hired. I was to work unpaid for the first two years of training, and I would receive a small salary after that. Mother made arrangements for me to sleep at my cousins' home and eat my meals at the restaurant. It was agreed that I would start the following Sunday morning, and we went home so my mother could pack my clothes.

That Sunday morning, I took the train to Kassa, a beautiful city with a population of over a hundred thousand people and a vibrant community of sixteen thousand Jews. There were two large and many smaller synagogues, as well as several Hebrew schools, to serve the needs of the Jewish community. There was a large cathedral, an opera house, and a tram line. The main street had beautiful shops and apartment buildings and hotels with coffeehouses. It was very exciting for me to be a part of city life, but at the same time, I felt some apprehension. I was only thirteen and a half years old, facing a new adventure on my own.

That first day, I left my suitcase at the restaurant and walked to the fur shop, which was close by. The owner placed me under the guidance of a young man who was eighteen or nineteen years old and in his fourth year of apprenticeship. This man became my teacher, and I, as a new apprentice, had to follow his orders. The fur shop was quite large, with a storefront and a workshop behind it. There were ten or so workers engaged in different tasks; some cut pelts such as Persian lamb or mink or fox, while others sewed these pieces together. There were three fireplaces to keep the workshop warm in the winter. In the mornings, my job was to remove the ashes and the cinders and start a new fire. Throughout the day, I had to keep adding charcoal to keep the flames going. In the evenings, I swept the floor, dusted, and covered the sewing machines, and did any other cleaning that was needed. The hardest job I had was to clean fur coats that were brought in for repairs. The cleaning process required me to mix sawdust with benzene in a bucket. To be cleaned, the fur coats were laid out on a table, and I had to take handfuls of this mixture and spread it on the fur, rubbing it into every inch until the coats shined. The benzene dried my skin and made my hands crack and bleed. It was very painful, and when my mother saw how damaged my hands had become, she bought me cotton gloves to wear for protection.

Once I got to know the city better, I was trusted to deliver the furs to different clients. Each coat had a label attached with the client's name, address, and apartment number. With two armfuls of fur coats, I would get on the streetcar and get off at various stops, ringing the bell for the different apartments. Once I had delivered the coats, I received a tip for my services, which gave me some spending money and a feeling of independence. Some six months after I started working, my boss (the older apprentice) began to show me how to sew pieces of fur together. He also showed me how to recognize and match the different patterns and colours so that the finished coat would look like one uniform piece rather than a patchwork.

Every Friday afternoon at 2 p.m., I was permitted to go home for the Sabbath. I grabbed my suitcase with my dirty clothes, went to the railway station, and took the train for home. On Friday evenings I met my friends at synagogue and told them about my adventures in the big city, and how much money I had made in tips that week. My apprenticeship lasted for approximately two years, until March 1944.

CHAPTER 5

A Year of Death and Birth

During the winter months of 1943, Aunt Bella became ill. She was no longer able to sit in her chair because of an infection on her thighs caused by remaining seated for approximately forty years. She was bedridden and the infection soon spread, which caused her other severe problems. My father's first cousin Dr. Emil Davidovits, a well-known doctor in Kassa, drove down twice a week to attend to her, but he was very clear that she would not be cured. In May she fell into a coma, dying one week later at home.

I was sad to see her laid out and covered with a sheet in our grandparents' quarters. This was the first member of my family whose death I had experienced. The ladies' burial society came to wash her and put her in a shroud. My grandfather, my father, and my uncle made a simple casket of lumber and the body was laid into it. The casket was loaded onto a horse-drawn cart and taken to the cemetery, followed by a procession of family and friends. But for some reason unknown to me, children were not allowed to attend. Bella's death left a huge hole in our lives, and my brothers and I felt a tremendous loss with her passing. I missed sitting on her lap and hearing the stories she read to us, which she had done for so many years. In retrospect, I'm relieved she was spared the events still to come.

As we grappled with Aunt Bella's death, it became obvious that my mother was approximately five months pregnant. At first I had mixed feelings, because there would be such a large gap in age between the baby and me. I was also concerned about how we would take care of another addition to our family without Anna to help. I was never home during the week, and my father had rejoined the labour battalions. We were stretched to our limits, but I had no say in this matter.

On June 28, 1943, my mother went into labour, and I was told to get the midwife then go to the doctor and inform him that he was going to be needed. I saw my grandmother and Aunt Irene heating water in pots and bringing linen into my mother's bedroom to prepare for the delivery. The labour and birth were difficult, but some hours later we were told that we could go in and see the new baby. She was a beautiful girl with brown hair and dark eyes, and her name was Judit. Although the family was happy, it was a time of tremendous turmoil for us and our community. It was not a good time for a Jewish mother to give birth or a Jewish child to be born.

In December 1943, we celebrated Chanukah, the festival of lights. My father managed to come home to celebrate with us in a year when we had lost our dear Bella and welcomed our little sister, Judit. Little did we know that this would be the final Chanukah we would mark together in our home.

CHAPTER 6

The Final Seder

By 1944, we were into the fifth year of the war. We'd faced so many difficulties during the previous years—intolerance, being treated as second-class citizens, the absence of my father and other young Jewish men from the town, our own abortive deportation—but we were still hanging on to the hope that the war would soon come to an end. We had severely rationed food supplies and materials for clothing. We had to gather all scrap metals and deliver them to the authorities to be used for the war effort, and store shelves were empty of staple products such as sugar, salt, and other condiments. In hindsight, we Hungarian Jews still lived in blissful ignorance amid all these inconveniences. We were not aware of the tragedy that had befallen other European Jews—those who were carted off in cattle cars to the six death camps in occupied Poland, or shot in pits and ravines in Ukraine and Belarus by the Einsatzgruppen.

In March 1944, the fascist Arrow Cross Party came to power in Hungary; its leader, Ferenc Szálasi, was a virulent Jew-hater. The Jewish community now faced critical problems, and the authorities strictly enforced the edict that all Jews had to wear a yellow Star of David on their chests. Bearing the star, I felt both demeaned and excluded. We were now a visible minority group, which added additional punishment to our discomforts. In spite of this, we maintained our concentration on the upcoming holiday of Pesach (Passover). By some miracle, my father and uncle were given a one-week furlough from their labour battalion at this special time.

The preparations for Passover started about one month prior to the first dinner, known as a Seder. The house was cleaned and scrubbed from top to bottom, all clothing was hung outside to air, and pockets were turned inside out to make sure there were no bread products or crumbs left. For eight days, we ate matzah (a thin cracker) instead of leavened bread to commemorate the flight of the Israelites from Egypt, when the bread dough they were making had no time to rise. We had special dishes used only on Passover, and we brought them down from the attic to be washed and cleaned. Unlike some other families, we had plentiful food available from our farm, including chickens and geese. There was a wonderful aroma of cooking and baking for the first two nights, and we recited the story of the Exodus, when the Israelites went from slavery in Egypt to freedom.

The ceremonial dinner always starts with the youngest child asking four questions: "On all other nights we eat bread or matzah, while on this night we eat only matzah? On all other nights we eat all kinds of vegetables and herbs, but on this night we have to eat bitter herbs? On all other nights we don't dip our vegetables in salt water, but on this night we dip them in it twice? On all other nights we eat while sitting upright, but on this night our elders eat while reclining?" After the questions have been recited, the elders answer them. Throughout history, the Jewish people have borne the brunt of persecutions in countries throughout the world, so we take time to remember these events. When telling the story of the exodus from Egypt, we also invite all those who are hungry to come and join us at our table.

I will always remember our final Seder; it is deeply etched in my memory. I remember my entire family seated around a beautifully set table—my grandfather and grandmother; my father and mother; my uncle Eugene and aunt Irene; my two younger siblings, Eugene and Alfred; and baby Judit in her crib. The candles burned in their candelabra, the beautiful dishes were laid out, and the heads of the family—my grandfather, my father, and my uncle—were leaning on cushions to symbolize relaxation and freedom from slavery in Egypt. After the reading and singing of the story, we had a dinner of several courses that lasted about four hours. For us, this was our last supper together.

When everything was cleared away, we washed the dishes and made preparations for the second Seder the following night. Around midnight, we went out into our yard to get some air before retiring. It was a balmy night, and the three elders were discussing the progression of the war on the Eastern Front. They hoped that the Soviet army would liberate us in five or six months. We thought the end of the war was very near, and we had no idea that something terrible was looming on the horizon. We retired to bed shortly after twelve with plans to wake up at a leisurely time the next morning, go to synagogue, and have the second Seder dinner after that.

At 2 a.m., we awoke to the sound of somebody knocking on the gates of the compound. As usual, these gates were locked for the night. Farkas, our guardian, was barking furiously. This was an unusual intrusion, and my father leaned out the window to see who was there. By this time, the entire household had been awakened by the commotion. I heard someone tell my father to come and open the gates so that he could enter with his horses and wagon. He said he needed to speak to my father urgently, so the gates were opened. The visitor turned out to be the forester from the area; we knew him well and trusted him. When my father still owned the pub, this man was a frequent customer, and he also had regular business dealings with my grandfather. By this point, everybody was intrigued by the forester's urgent need to speak with us, so he was brought to my grandparents' quarters. There, he told us that he had just come from the pub, where he'd overheard several gendarmes say they were planning to gather all the Jews of the town and its vicinity and remove them from their homes the next day. He insisted that we get into his wagon immediately; he would take us away and find us a secure place to hide in the forest. We were all speechless.

The elders talked it over, and after a lengthy discussion my grandfather decided that because it was Passover and the Sabbath, we could not travel unless our lives were in imminent danger, and no one could have imagined such a threat. The man begged us, but to no avail. Eventually he drove away, and the gates were locked behind him.

After this episode, I lay awake in my bed. I felt that we must do something, but Grandfather's decisions were law and had to be respected. The memories of our near deportation in 1942 were spinning around in my head. This could not be happening again!

At about 6 a.m. the following morning, two gendarmes forced open the gates and entered our living quarters. They yelled that we had five minutes to pack a bundle before being taken away. They said that we should hand over any money or jewellery, because where we were going we would have no need for it. My mother grabbed my little sister in her arms and told us to put on layers of clothing. Father told us to put on our winter boots, and then he went to our grandparents' quarters to see how they were doing. We packed as much food as we could into backpacks. Mother was busy worrying about what to pack to sustain a family of six for an unknown journey of an unknown length. All the while, the gendarmes were harassing us and rifling through our dressers to see what they could take from us. I had several binders filled with my stamp collection, which I was sad to leave behind. Again, my thoughts went to the last deportation, and I was consumed with fear of what was to come. All this time Farkas was barking nonstop, as if he knew something terrible was happening.

In these final moments, our neighbour Ily, a Christian lady who was a good friend of ours, came rushing into our home. The gendarmes yelled at her to get out, saying it was not her concern, but she refused to go. She turned to my mother and said, "Ethel, where are you taking the baby? Why don't you leave her with me?" Mother refused the offer. I wonder to this day what would have become of Judit had my mother accepted. Immediately, the gendarmes forcibly removed our three families from the house. We struggled to carry our bundles, and my grandmother could hardly lift hers. As I left, I said a silent and devastated goodbye to my home, to the orchard, and to Farkas. My gut told me that this deportation would be more serious than the one in 1942, because this time we were all being taken away. Who would take care of our home while we were gone?

All our neighbours watched as the three Eisen families walked with our bundles, guarded by gendarmes. Some of them yelled and spat at us as we passed. We walked to the public school at the centre of town, approximately a kilometre away. Normally, they would escort criminals to jail in this fashion. I felt ashamed, and yet we hadn't committed any crimes. When we arrived at the school, other Jewish families greeted us, and by the end of the day, all ninety families were there. We talked anxiously, contemplating what our fates might be. The gendarmes divided us into two rooms, with at least two hundred people crammed together in each. We were only a twenty- or twenty-five-minute walk from our homes and the comfort of our beds, but instead we were sitting on the floor of the school. We began to realize that we were no longer the masters of our own destiny. The gendarmes had sealed us off from the rest of the town as if we were pariahs.

That night in the school was the first of many disturbing nights to come. With over two hundred people squeezed together on the floor, it was nearly impossible to be polite. Some people tried to sleep, but there were babies crying nonstop. The discomfort of the space and a general sense of nervousness and fear took hold, and many complained. The facilities in the school were very basic—only a communal outhouse and some pails of water for washing. In the morning, people stirred and tried to stand up, but every inch of floor space was occupied and there was no room to move. I thought about the Passover meal, and the special coffee and breakfast I had been waiting for all year. I recalled the aroma that permeated the house when I ground the beans. All year I waited for this genuine coffee (the rest of the year we drank coffee made from ground chicory). If we were at home, I thought, I'd be eating matzah broken into little pieces and covered with hot coffee, milk, and sugar. Instead, I was in the school with an empty stomach and a terrible day ahead of me.

In the morning, the gendarmes ordered us to assemble with our bundles in the schoolyard. This would be the first step in our journey from relative freedom to slavery and an unknown destiny. From there, almost five hundred Jewish people were marched en masse from the centre of town to the railway station. Rabbi Tannenbaum, the spiritual leader of our community, was ordered to head the group. He was an older gentleman with a long white beard, and his wife, who was an invalid, had to be carried on a chair by her two sons. Mothers carried their babies in their arms because carriages and strollers were not permitted. On both sides of the road, the townspeople jeered and cursed at us as we passed. Many were looking out the windows of the Jewish homes they now occupied. I thought to myself how disgusting it was for our neighbours to behave this way. Many townsfolk who bought goods on credit from Jews like my grandfather were happy they wouldn't have to pay the money back. Our deportation was an economic windfall for them.

As we walked by our own property, we could see that someone had occupied our home overnight. Farkas seemed to sense that we were among the group, and he barked through the fence as if wailing to say goodbye. To me, Farkas was more humane than the townspeople, because he was the only one who seemed to care that we were being taken away.

By the time we arrived at the railway station, some of the elderly people could hardly stand. This station was small and could barely accommodate our group. Eventually, we were told to board the train to Kassa. Everyone was full of questions. When were we going to come back? Were we going to see our homes again? Would we again live a normal life? After about an hour and a half, we arrived in Kassa and walked from the station to a nearby synagogue with a large yard. Members of the Jewish community met us there and placed us with Jewish families in the town. My family went to stay with the parents of Emil Davidovitch, the doctor who took care of Aunt Bella. They lived in a three-bedroom apartment that now had to accommodate ten additional people. We slept on the floor on mattresses that had to be cleared away in the morning. It was difficult to replenish our food supply, but we managed by cutting back on our intake. Although we were no longer guarded by the gendarmes, we weren't permitted to leave the area we lived in and roam the town. Living in these close quarters was not ideal, and we wondered how long we would have to stay there.

Rumours began spreading through the community that a place was being built to house the thirty thousand or so Jews from our province, but we didn't quite know where this place would be. Half this number lived in the city of Kassa itself, and almost the same number in the rest of the province; therefore, they would need a very large area to house all of us. Within a week of our arrival, posted notices began to appear, directing the Jewish inhabitants on several streets to gather their belongings and walk to a brickyard on the outskirts of the city. Those affected needed to be there on the day designated on the order; disobedience would result in harsh punishment.

This announcement shattered our seemingly secure life once again, and now we knew we would be moving to another unknown place. Each day we checked which streets were to be moved out, and when we didn't see ours, we always felt a bit of relief. But we knew we had to be ready to move on a day's notice, and so we had to purchase in advance whatever provisions we could get. Our clothing had to be clean and we had to reassess how much we would be able to carry. We would keep only the most important items because the walk to the brickyard was approximately two kilometres. This period of waiting was very nerve-racking, and we were constantly reconsidering what we should take and what we should leave behind.

Finally they posted the order for our street. We collected our bundles and said our goodbyes to yet another place that had sheltered us. The streets outside were filled with Jewish people, young and old, struggling with their loads—all headed in the same direction. We were not permitted to hire a taxi or a horse-drawn cart, so it took us several hours to reach the brickyard. We entered through a gate guarded by gendarmes and saw thousands of people milling around. We were taken to a large shed that was used for drying bricks. Red dust covered the rough floor and was constantly raised by people's movements. There were hundreds of people in our shed and no affordances for privacy, but we staked out an area where we made our home. My father, my uncle, and I went outside to familiarize ourselves with the layout of the brickyard. Before we even saw it, we could smell the terrible fumes from the communal outdoor latrine, where people sat on a wooden board balanced over a large pit full of excrement. The entire brickyard was surrounded by barbed wire and guarded by gendarmes.

We received a bowl of soup daily. There appeared to be only one available water tap to serve the needs of thousands of people. The food that we had brought with us dwindled quickly, and we, like everyone else, soon faced a pervasive hunger. To try to relieve that, I would regularly join other teenagers at the main gate to volunteer for cleanup duty. Each day, the gendarmes chose about fifty boys to march to the town to clean up former Jewish areas so that the non-Jewish population could move in. For this work, we were given a piece of bread. I cannot remember how my mother took care of the baby, but she was still breastfeeding her when we arrived in Kassa. She could no longer care for the family as she always had, and I wondered how this made her feel.

We stayed in this horrible brickyard for about three weeks. Every day around noon, an SS officer would arrive and we would gather around to listen to his speech. He told us that we would be resettled in the east, that our families would be together, and that we would be working on farms. Every day for five days, the SS officer repeated the same speech—this, I later learned, was a brainwashing tactic used by the Nazis so they would be able to load us into the cattle cars with ease. We couldn't wait to leave that horrible place, and anything else sounded better than where we were.

During the officer's speeches, I thought often of my mother's family, who were deported from Slovakia in 1942. The postcard they'd sent us said they were all together and were working on farms, waiting eagerly for our arrival. We all hoped that we would meet up with our beautiful cousins and extended family in Lublin district. In truth, the Nazis, those masters of lies and deception, had tricked us into believing that our relatives were still alive. Their real aim was to convince us to enter the cattle cars willingly and peacefully. For us, living in such horrible conditions in the brickyard, the promise of future work on spacious farms was welcome news.

CHAPTER 7

The Train

In the spring of 1944, three weeks after we'd arrived in the brickyard, the Nazis began to liquidate this temporary transit camp. Several transports had already left for the "east." I was chosen with some others to clean up the sheds where the deportees had been housed. I found coins and other articles that people had left behind—only the coins were of value to me. My family and I were told to get ready for the third transport. We also had to leave behind valuable possessions because we knew that the cramped space in a cattle car would not allow for any extra baggage besides our minimal personal belongings.

I was preoccupied with thoughts of the past. I remembered how, in 1942, my mother, my aunt, my siblings, and I were taken to the Karpathian Mountains and later sent home. This time, I was cognizant that there were additional members of our family on the transport—my grandfather; my grandmother, who was quite feeble; my nine-month-old sister, Judit—and I was very concerned about how we were all going to handle travelling in the cramped conditions of the first two transports I had seen being loaded.

On the day of our departure, we picked up our meagre bundles and were taken to the loading area, where the cattle cars were waiting. There, we were met by the Hungarian gendarmes. After we were loaded into the cars, the train set off from the brickyard, which was in a suburb of Kassa, to the main railway station a short distance away. Once there, each car was given a pail of drinking water and an empty pail to use as a toilet. Then the doors were closed and bolted down. My gut told me we were in danger. What was happening to us and where were we going to end up?

In my childhood, trains represented stability. Every morning, when I heard the whistle of the train that brought distant students to my town, I knew it was time to walk to school with my friends. And every afternoon, the train whistled again as it took the students back to their homes, signalling that school was out. The train also took me away on summer holidays to my mother's family's farm in Kolbašov; my uncle Herman was always waiting at the station with a carriage and two prancing horses. I would sit on the buckboard beside him and take the reins—such an exuberant and liberating feeling.

The contrast between those happy memories and my departure from the brickyard on this transport couldn't have been more pronounced. One hundred people and their bundles were crammed into each car. We were stuck together, standing room only, and could hardly breathe properly because the heat generated by our bodies made the air unbearable. The situation was dehumanizing, debilitating, and devastating, both psychologically and physically. There was only a small barred opening near the ceiling for ventilation. The water was gone almost immediately, and it was never replaced. The toilet pail was not emptied because the door was never opened, and the stench infused the entire car. Our bundles of belongings, left on the floor, were also overrun with waste.

I couldn't get close to my parents and they couldn't protect me. I felt alone, overwhelmed by the stench of urine and fecal matter. I couldn't relieve myself because the car was so tightly packed and lacked privacy. The moans of people who were claustrophobic or in pain were very unsettling. When I relive these memories today, I have nightmarish thoughts about my mother, who was holding my still-breastfeeding nine-month-old sister. I can't imagine how she managed without food and water. My two younger brothers, only eight and ten years old, must have found it terrifying to be squeezed and surrounded by taller people.

Some things I will never forget about the journey: the smell of smoke, the sound of the locomotive as it built up steam to pull the thirty to forty loaded cars, the clicking of the wheels as they hit the joints of the rails. On the first day, the train stopped to refuel with coal and water for the locomotive. We screamed out to our guards, begging for water for ourselves. They told us to throw out jewellery in exchange. Some discussion took place, and soon several people threw pieces of hidden jewellery through a small opening in the car. Once the gendarmes got the valuables, they simply walked away without honouring their promise. That first night in the car, I fell asleep standing up, lulled by the rhythm of the train. I awoke suddenly to the sound of the locomotive's loud whistle; I thought I'd had a nightmare, but in reality I was living the nightmare.

As the sun's rays penetrated the opening the next morning, I felt somewhat better and thought there might still be some hope. But at the next stop, the person nearest to the small barred window, in the upper corner of the car, was hoisted up to see where we were. He told us the name of the station and we realized that we were now in occupied Poland, a shocking revelation because we'd expected to be resettled in the east. The feelings of desperation worsened. We travelled on for a second night and two people died. Their bodies remained in the car with us.

The crying babies could no longer be heard by the third night, when the train finally came to a stop. Through the opening, we heard people speaking German. The cars were shuffled back and forth, and as the steel bumpers hit each other, a shock wave went through the entire train. We were all awake, a miserable bundle of human cargo.

CHAPTER 8

Arrival in Auschwitz II–Birkenau

fter three days of travel, I heard the doors of the other cattle cars being opened. I couldn't wait for ours to open too. Nothing could be worse, I thought, than what I had experienced those three days, locked up in a living tomb. Finally, someone lifted the latch of our cattle car and the door was opened. Light flooded in, and people began moving about like dormant larvae stimulated by a sudden shock of light and noise. It was as if bright light had penetrated into a dark cave, forcing everyone inside to awaken from a three-day coma. A man wearing a striped cap, jacket, and pants yelled, *"Raus schnell!"* I knew some German, and I understood this to mean "Get out fast!" I thought any person who wore this sort of garb must be a criminal. Did they think *we* were criminals? Surely this was a mistake. *"Raus schnell!"* I wanted to move, but I couldn't. I wanted to find my bundle, but everything was covered in human waste.

I was among the first pulled out of our cattle car, and my legs could hardly hold me up. I saw more men in striped outfits, as well as SS soldiers and officers dressed in sharp and shiny

Auschwitz II–Birkenau, showing the train ramp, four crematoria with gas chambers, fire pit, and the arrival ramp.

The guardhouse and entrance to Auschwitz II–Birkenau.

uniforms. Other people were also hauled out of the car, including my mother with my baby sister in her arms, my grandparents, and my uncle and aunt. We were all numb from the shock of the journey, and confused by the harsh orders that were being barked at us.

At the end of the platform there was a plume of fire, and I thought we were at some kind of factory. I recognized the same odour I smelled at home whenever the blacksmith put a burning shoe on a horse's hoofs, and I concluded it was burning flesh. Beyond the floodlit platform, all was dark. The men in the striped outfits told us that our bundles would be delivered to us the next day. Forcefully and systematically, they separated the men and women into two columns. All older males and children were sent over to the women's line. The men in the striped outfits kept telling us that we would see each other in the morning. There were no goodbyes spoken here.

I found myself in the men's line with my father and my uncle. My grandfather, my grandmother, my mother (still holding baby Judit), my two younger siblings, and my aunt were all marched away in the other group. Everything happened swiftly and we had no time to think. I didn't have an opportunity to speak to my mother—nor did our eyes ever meet—and I wasn't able to say goodbye to her. We simply moved forward in a single column toward an SS officer wearing white gloves. He looked at each person and indicated with a flick of his hands whether that person should go right or left. My father went first, then my uncle, and then me. He sent me to the same group as my father and uncle. We were guarded by SS soldiers and marched through a forest of birch trees with the other selected men. Along the way, I observed a large fire at ground level some distance away, and from my perspective it seemed that people were jumping into the flames. When I asked my father if this could be possible, he quickly told me to keep quiet and continue walking. We entered a building called the Sauna, where more men in striped outfits ordered us to hand over any remaining documents and jewellery, and then told us to strip naked. They took our clothes away but permitted us to keep our boots.

In the next stage of processing, our hair was cut from our heads, underarms, and groins by yet more men in striped uniforms. They had numbers and triangles printed on strips of cloth and sewn on their jackets. The man in charge of this unit wore a band on his arm that said "Kapo" (boss). The Kapo lined up the older people and had his men check if any had gold crowns or fillings in their teeth. Those who did were taken aside, and their teeth were extracted on the spot with a pair of pliers. Meanwhile, the rest of us were ordered to bend over to have our rectums checked for hidden items.

The next stage was the showers. I had never seen a shower before in my life, and I was in awe of the installation. There were numerous showerheads and large wheels that controlled the flow of the hot and cold water. Although I had been in a *mikvah* (ritual bath) at home, it was intimidating to be in a large group of naked strangers. We had to lay our boots on the edge of the shower while we bathed; my father, my uncle, and I kept a good eye on ours because we had custom-made boots that would last for a long time. Suddenly, the Kapo and his helpers started to collect them. My father warned us when he saw this, and we quickly grabbed our boots and kept them under our arms while we showered. Had we lost those boots, our lives would have been even more at risk—if your feet were not protected, you would be unable to work and would be selected for gassing. Those who lost theirs were lucky if they got a pair of wooden clogs instead. These clogs were more like a piece of wood with a canvas top stapled to it, and they were damaging to the feet. Our boots were treasures that we had to guard day and night.

The cruelty of the SS guards first became apparent in the shower room. While we were washing, a soldier stood by one of the big wheels that controlled the water temperature. For sport, he turned it on to scalding. As we tried to jump away to avoid getting burned, another soldier with a truncheon would beat us to get back under the flow. Then the first soldier turned the water freezing cold.

A young man who was showering with us held his eyeglasses in his hands. They had very thick lenses and he was obviously short-sighted. The rush of water washed his glasses right out of his grasp, and when he got down on his knees to try to find them, a guard came over and kicked him in the side of the head with his jackboot. The young man rolled over and the guard stomped on his chest. I could hear the cracking of ribs. The guard, who was now in a frenzy, continued to stomp on the man until he was dead. The rest of us carried on washing as if nothing had happened, but I was shocked and terrified. To this day, I can't figure out what precipitated the guard's horrible act. Perhaps he thought seeing a naked man on his hands and knees was comical, and he wanted to humiliate him.

After the showers, we were marched to our barracks with our boots on but without any clothes. Inside there were rows of triple-tier bunks with no mattresses or blankets. After three days of standing in the cattle car, it felt wonderful to lie down in a horizontal position, even if it was on wooden planks. I tried to process the events of the few hours since our arrival, but I couldn't understand the evil of these guards. I was worried about what the future had in store for me. I felt numb. This was my initiation to Auschwitz-Birkenau.

* * *

I was awoken suddenly from my short sleep to loud banging and shouts of "*Raus schnell!*" We were on the top bunk. Father jumped down first, then me, and then finally my uncle. The Kapos ordered us out of the barracks. It was a beautiful, sunny morning and I found myself looking at hundreds of barracks, thousands of emaciated people behind barbed-wire fences, and dozens of guard towers where SS soldiers manned machine guns and searchlights. Nearby, there were four huge chimneys belching angry red flames and smoke. The smell of burning flesh that had first overwhelmed me when I exited the cattle car still permeated the air. I could not fathom the immense size of this place, and I thought that we must be in a large industrial area. My father told me to move fast if I heard the Kapo's orders, because otherwise they would beat me.

Tables were set up in front of our barracks, and two men sat at each one. They ordered us to come to the table nearest us in single file. Again, my father went first, I was next, and my uncle was last. The first man asked my name, my place and date of birth, what languages I spoke, my height and weight, and the colour of my hair. The next man tattooed a number on my left arm: A-9892. My father's number was A-9891 and my uncle's was A-9893. Wherever we went, I was always between them; they were my guardian angels.

Nearby, there were piles of striped pants, jackets, and caps. I was handed one of each and put them on, but they didn't fit well. We had no socks or underwear, no belt or suspenders to hold up our pants. From a pile of unattended dirty rags, my father managed to find a pair of trousers, and with his teeth and fingers he ripped off strips of material that he twisted into belts for me, my uncle, and himself. We stripped more pieces of cloth and wrapped them around our feet in place of socks. We also kept a small piece to use as a wipe in lieu of toilet paper. My father and uncle were inventive, and they taught me how to survive under these horrific conditions.

Once I put on these striped prisoner's clothes, I felt like I was no longer a human being, only a number. On two strips of white material, prisoner workers stamped a Star of David with my number. As we proceeded down the line, they used needle and thread to stitch one strip on the front left side on the jacket and the other on the back. Different groups had different triangles: political prisoners got a red triangle (with a *P* for Polish or *F* for French, etc.), Roma people had a brown triangle, Jehovah's Witnesses a violet triangle, homosexuals a pink triangle, habitual criminals a green triangle, and so-called asocials a black triangle. Out of all these groups, we Jews were on the lowest rung of the ladder in the camp hierarchy.

Soon, two prisoners arrived carrying a large canister of hot tea, my first food or drink in days. They gave us metal dishes, lined us up, and portioned out the tea. It tasted quite different from what I was used to at home. My father asked these men if we would see our families that day. They laughed at him, pointed to one of the chimneys spewing flames, and asked, "Where did you come from?"

My father replied, "We arrived from Hungary in the middle of the night."

The prisoner said, "It's 1944 and you don't know what this place is all about? Your families have gone up through the chimney." This was camp vernacular to describe being gassed and cremated.

At that moment, I'm sure Father realized that my mother and the rest of our family had been murdered soon after our arrival, but it took me a few days to understand the processes of this killing machine. Until I learned more about the existence of the gas chambers, I assumed that they had been burned alive. I was devastated, but I was under such threat at every moment that I could not dwell on the loss of my family during the day. I could think only of work, food, and physical survival. My father and uncle never spoke of the deaths, so when I thought of my family while I lay in my bunk at night, I was alone with my grief. In truth, it was easier to exist in a state of denial than to face this horrible reality.

After the prison workers tattooed our numbers on our left arms and inscribed them on our clothing, they lined us up once more. An officer yelled out, "Doctors and lawyers, raise your hands!" Those who did were ordered to step out of the formation and were taken away. Next, he asked for farmers. Many of us raised our hands. My father knew from his time in the labour battalions that working on a farm would give us access to potatoes, turnips, or beets. The guards selected a hundred men, including the three of us.

I was hungry, thirsty, and completely shocked by how my life was changing minute by minute and hour by hour. Everything about this place was threatening and filled me with fear, and now we were told that we were going to a different camp. I wondered if the new camp would be similar to Birkenau.

The guards marched us several kilometres down the road to Auschwitz I. En route, we passed a group of women with shaved heads and striped dresses; they were harnessed to a huge cement roller that they pulled to grade the road. Some had dilapidated shoes, some wooden clogs or sandals, and some were barefoot. The SS women guards were whipping them and yelling, "*Schnell! Faster, you damn Jews!*" The soles of the feet of the women without shoes had been ripped to shreds, and the rocks they walked upon were covered with their blood. The SS women were large and bursting out of their uniforms, and the contrast between them and their skeletal prisoners was striking. I couldn't help wondering if we would be treated the same way.

CHAPTER 9

Arbeit Macht Frei

Our group of about one hundred men arrived at Auschwitz I in early May 1944 with only one cup of tea in our bellies. We entered the camp through a large metal gate with the words "*Arbeit macht frei*" (Work sets you free) overtop of it. Near the gate, there was a guardhouse bustling with SS soldiers and attack dogs. My first glimpse of the barbed-wire fences and the prison-like red-brick buildings sent shudders down my spine. Once we passed through the gate, I looked to the right and saw an all-male orchestra. These men played marching music when we left for work in the morning and again when we returned in the evening. I was uplifted by the sound of the music, and my body responded to its tempo. How could such beautiful music coexist with the ominous camp in the background?

Auschwitz I had twenty-eight two-storey brick barracks. Each floor was divided into two parts, and and there were a total of twelve hundred inmates per barrack. Each building had a Block Altester (barracks elder), and each room had a room elder. The elders were part of the camp bureaucracy, and they enjoyed certain privileges, including privacy and extra provisions. The washroom in each barracks (one washroom per building) had a trough with many water taps that could accommodate a large number of people at a time, and next to this trough was a room full of flush toilets. We slept in triple-tiered bunk beds, as we had at Birkenau, but now we had mattresses instead of wooden slats. The mattresses had once been filled with straw, but after years of use by previous prisoners, they were now bags of dust. On top of each mattress sat a smelly, dirty blanket.

Our work unit occupied one room on the second floor of barrack 16, and my bed was on the top of the bunk closest to the roofline, which was covered with small tiles made of some kind of shavings that were glued together. We had no extra items. My total wardrobe consisted of my jacket, my pants, my cap, and my boots. Here I began my new life as a slave labourer working for the German Reich.

Near the main camp gate was a long kitchen building where prisoners prepared meals for approximately twenty-five thousand inmates and the SS guards. Those twenty-five thousand inmates occupied approximately twenty of the barracks, and several others were used as warehouses for clothing and wool blankets that were confiscated from people when they arrived at Birkenau. These items were cleaned at Auschwitz I and eventually shipped to Germany for their economic benefit. One barracks was used as a first aid clinic where people with work-related injuries came for help. Barrack 21 housed a surgery, and the upper floors were used as hospital wards for patients. Next to barrack 21 was the building used for medical experiments on inmates. Barrack 11 had torture chambers and prison cells; beside it, there was a firing wall where seventy thousand of the earliest Auschwitz inmates—mostly Polish political prisoners—were shot. I always gave barrack 11 a wide berth. On the other side of barrack 21 was the laundry building. Auschwitz I also had a small experimental crematory, called Crematorium I.

Arriving at Auschwitz I the first time, we were taken to a barracks where a Kapo, who introduced himself as Heinrich, was waiting for us. He was short and wore a green triangle—he was most likely a murderer from a German jail who had been released and brought to the camp to be our work boss. He and others like him turned out to be the most brutal killers in the camp. The SS gave them permission to beat and kill any workers they pleased. He had a truncheon in his hand and piercing eyes that seemed to look right through you. Speaking in German, he said, "If you do not follow my orders, your life will come to a speedy end. I will beat you to death. You will die here from beating or starvation, or be worked to death. And surely you will go through the gas chamber. This unit is called the Landwirtschaft Kommando [Land Management Unit]. Tomorrow morning you will have your first taste of Auschwitz." I could understand and communicate in basic German, which I had studied briefly in school and heard my grandfather occasionally speak at home. After the Kapo's introduction, we were abruptly dismissed.

Because we were not allowed to enter our barracks until all units had returned from work, we had a few hours to walk around and familiarize ourselves with the layout of the camp. I observed that the Kapos and some other inmates appeared to have tailor-made prisoner clothing and sturdy, smart-looking boots. They also looked well fed compared to the other prisoners, who were skinny and haggard. Most of these inmates bore red triangles printed with a *P*; they were political prisoners and the first inmates in Auschwitz I. They were called the Prominente, and they controlled the entire internal infrastructure of the camp. Eventually it became evident to me that the hierarchy in the camp gave political prisoners certain benefits to keep body and soul together, while we Jews on the lowest rung of the ladder had to fight for survival on a daily basis. I knew that unless a door opened, there would be no way for me to climb out of this hole. Starting the very next morning, our lives were controlled by an iron discipline every hour of the day and night.

The orchestra suddenly struck up a tune, and we went over to the gate to watch the prisoners coming back from their work. I enjoyed hearing the music, and for a moment, I thought that I was somewhere else–and that I was free. The work units, one hundred per group, came marching through the gate in rows of five. The head of the unit reported the number of prisoners to a guard; this ensured that the same number of people who left in the morning also returned in the evening. These men worked in ammunition factories and at construction sites. It took over two hours for all the units to march back to camp.

We hurried back to our barracks, which was now filled with very tired, hungry, and aggressive men. I felt like I was in the Tower of Babel, hearing my barrack-mates speak so many different languages. The men rushed to the washing facility to clean themselves and rinse out their jackets and pants. The barracks elder tried to ensure that we stayed as clean as possible, because if we didn't, lice could easily multiply and spread typhus. Signs in the washing area depicted lice with their ugly limbs and read, "One louse could be the end of your life." The men wrung out their clothes and put them back on while still wet. Nobody had any towels. Their boots were also cleaned of mud, and black axle grease was applied to them from a bucket that stood nearby, in order to give them the appearance of cleanliness. In Auschwitz I, it was possible to keep yourself fairly clean, and this was good for my morale.

We then all lined up for our so-called dinner, which consisted of a cup of watery coffee, a thin slice of bread, and a tiny square of margarine. This was my first dinner in Auschwitz I. It was not nearly enough calories to nurture our bodies. My father, my uncle, and I discussed whether to consume the whole slice of bread now or leave some for the next day. Our dilemma was that we had no place to keep even this small portion of bread, and we knew that if given the opportunity, starving inmates would steal it from us, because hunger drove people to extreme measures.

The next morning, the order for the *appel* (roll call) sounded early. We all rushed downstairs and lined up in front of our barracks in a military fashion. Twenty rows of five people spread out so that the count could proceed smoothly. I extended my left hand sideways to touch the shoulder of the person next to me and my right hand straight ahead to touch the back of the person in front of me. We had to line up in this manner with great speed or the Kapos would beat us to a pulp. As the SS soldier in charge of our barracks arrived to take the count, the Kapo yelled, "*Mützen ab!*" (Caps off). This procedure was repeated in each of the twenty barracks.

We had to stand at full attention while the numbers were collated by the Lagerschreiber, an inmate who was in charge of gathering the tabulations and reporting them to the SS officer on duty. On a good day, when the totals were acceptable, *appel* would take anywhere from an hour to an hour and a half. When the numbers didn't add up, though, we could stand there for

83

hours while they checked the barracks, looking for someone who had died in his bunk. On these occasions, they brought the body down and physically held it up so the count could be completed. The Kapos would then yell out, "*Mützen auf!*" (Caps on).

Once the guards were satisfied, the orchestra started to play and each work unit marched toward the gate in a systematic and organized manner, led by its Kapo. We marched off at a fast pace as if we were a bunch of happy campers going to work for the Reich. Our Kommandant, Unterscharführer Kuntz, surrounded our column with guards and German shepherds, in front, in back, and on each side. After the ordeal of *appel*, it felt good to be able to walk and observe the scenery outside the camp. I didn't see any local civilians, and I eventually learned that the Nazis had cleared a large area to accommodate Auschwitz I, II, and III, as well as smaller satellite labour camps. Civilians were not allowed to enter this exclusion zone.

As we walked, we passed a bakery operated by inmates. It was baking bread for the camp and was bustling with prisoners loading loaves onto trucks. The air around it was thick with the tantalizing smell of baking bread. It made my stomach growl with hunger. Each day we passed this bakery on our way to work, and each day my stomach growled more than it had the day before. The tiny slice of bread we received each night was a terrible tease. I envied the fellows who loaded the bread trucks, because they would surely never go hungry like me.

As we walked on, we reached an area where both sides of the road were covered with mustard plants as far as the eye could see. They were waist-high and the flowers on top were bright yellow. We stopped at a large settlement with many barracks, horse stables, and all kinds of farm equipment. This was a satellite camp called Budy. Here many prisoners were doing different types of work. I was surprised to see a boy in his twenties from my home-town. We made eye contact, but we had no opportunity to speak. When I was ordered to load scythes on a flatbed cart, he came around and slipped me a piece of bread.

There were approximately fifty prisoners who lived and worked at Budy with their SS guards. They were all familiar with farm work and skilled at handling horses. The prisoners cared well for these beautiful animals, which were used to haul farm products and to till the land. Budy was a satellite camp in the middle of large farmlands, and it served as a distribution point for many crops, such as potatoes, beets, turnips, onions, hay, and fodder for cattle. (I even saw a huge pile of mouldy bread that eventually found its way into the soup we consumed for lunch.) The flatbed cart I was told to load was pulled and pushed to the edge of the mustard field, where approximately fifty of us set to work to cutting the plants. There was a big rush to choose a scythe that was not overly large. The bigger scythes had lar-ger blades but were quite heavy. The rush to get a smaller one quickly became dangerous—fifty men wielding these knife-like tools was quite a hazard. We also received a whetstone to sharpen the blades of the scythes. The Kommandant announced that if anyone broke his stone, it would be considered an act of sabotage and the offender would be shot on the spot.

The Kommandant was an Austrian farmer and he knew his work well. He had a meeting with our Kapo (who was more familiar with the inside of a German jail than farm work) and our under-Kapo (a Polish political prisoner named Stasek, who was a proficient farmer), and he explained how we should proceed and how large an area he expected us to complete by the end of the day. The strongest people would lead, setting the tempo for the rest to follow. Mustard stalks are quite thick and the height of the cut needed to be accurate, no more than three inches above the ground. The lead man began cutting, and when he was a few feet away (far enough that he would not injure anyone with his scythe), the next man started a fresh row, and so on. My father, my uncle, and I were familiar with scythes because my grandfather had used one for cutting hay. We knew the tool was most effective when held at a certain angle and an even height. We set off—I followed my father, and my uncle followed me. Throughout the day they encouraged me to keep up the pace. It was gruelling physical work and our Kapo watched constantly to make sure that we followed a steady rhythm. It was a hot day and the sun burned down on us; I was dehydrated, and there was no water available at the site. Auschwitz and its satellite camps were built in a climatically challenging area in Europe, between the Vistula and Soła Rivers with swamps all around. A hot and humid day without water was very hard on the body.

I had used a scythe at home for half an hour or sometimes an hour, but here I cut continuously for four hours until we stopped for lunch. I felt like my back was breaking; the palms of my hands had large blisters, and some had already burst. Yet despite all our hours of work, it looked as if we had hardly made a dent. My father told me that I must keep going or the Kapo would beat me, and he knew that repeated beatings would lessen my chance of survival. He told me that I must put one foot in front of the other and think good thoughts about surviving this ordeal. My father had always been a strict disciplinarian, and now that disciplined approach helped keep me focused and determined. I thought about my prior rebelliousness and my historically strained relationship with him. I'd always felt like I never measured up to his expectations in public school and Hebrew school. We were further estranged by his three-year absence in the labour battalions. But in these new circumstances at Auschwitz, I was very dependent on his emotional support, and I was extremely appreciative that I had my father and my uncle there with me. They did everything they could to keep me alive, and without them I would never have survived the first two weeks in that hellhole.

After our morning's labour, we stopped for a thirty-minute lunch break. A horse-drawn cart brought canisters of soup, and we each grabbed a metal dish and lined up in single file to be served. When my turn came, I received a ladle of a foul-smelling mixture I had never before seen in my life. It was dörgeműze, a type of vegetable soup. As I looked in the bowl, I recognized mouldy bread and cut-up stalks of mustard, and I simply refused to eat it. My father knew I must eat to survive, however, and he practically forced it down my throat. A few days later, when the hunger was more severe, the dörgeműze started to taste pretty good, and a single ladle was no longer enough to fill my stomach.

After everyone had received his portion of soup, there was sometimes extra left over. On those days, the man ladling the soup yelled out, "*Repeta!*" People would jump up and jostle one another to get to the front of the line. The Kapo often used this as an opportunity to have some sport, beating those men who'd made it to the front. Even worse, however, was the way the prisoners themselves would nearly kill each other when the soup was gone. I stood and watched as men dove into the canisters head-first to lick up every remaining drop. I had never seen people act in this way, like a pack of dogs fighting over a piece of meat. I was determined that no matter what happened, I would never stoop to that level.

One lunchtime, while the prisoners sat together in a tight group, the SS guards formed a cordon around us and sat in the shade of some trees. One of the guards closest to me unbuckled a knapsack, took out a sandwich and a Thermos, and proceeded to have his lunch. He washed down his large sandwich with the liquid from his Thermos, which I imagined must have contained good coffee. As a starving person, I found it terribly demeaning to watch the guards enjoy their generous meals in full view of us. While the guard ate, his big German shepherd sat motionless beside him, watching us with his ears perked up in guard mode. He was a beautiful dog, and he made me think of Farkas. What was he doing? Was he still guarding our house? The guard tore off a piece of his sandwich and threw it in front of the dog, but the dog sat on his haunches without a move. Suddenly, a member of our group jumped up and ran to grab this piece of bread. The guard uttered a simple order, and with one great leap, the dog had the man's wrist between his teeth. He kept hold of him until the guard gave him the order to release. The man's wrist was shredded, and he received a terrible beating as well. I wondered at the time who was crueller, the dog or the handler? At the end of the day, the man with the injured wrist and another with a severe cut were left behind at Budy, and we never saw them again.

After lunch, we continued to work for several hours, until finally we were ordered to stop and pile up our scythes on the flatbed cart, which was then brought back to Budy. Never in my life had I worked that hard for eight or nine hours a day on a starvation diet of approximately three hundred calories. I was hungry and tired, and we still had several kilometres to march back to Auschwitz. The Kapo drove us mercilessly, calling out, "Left, left, left," and constantly checking to see that we were all in step. As we neared Auschwitz, I could hear the camp orchestra and this perked me up. I regained some strength, and finally we arrived. Somehow, the marching and the music kept my spirits up. To me, the music was the only humane and normal thing in the camp. The music gave me hope.

We marched into camp looking forward to getting washed and with great anticipation of our meagre dinner. It is amazing how resilient the human body is—how we could survive on so few calories and adjust to so little food. As time went on, however, our bodies began to deteriorate due to the lack of nourishment. This was particularly evident when inmates contracted scurvy from a shortage of vitamins. On top of the hard daily labour, we had to deal with all these ailments and physical challenges, and still try to stay sane. I had a feeling of accomplishment that I managed to keep up with older and much stronger men.

At the end of every day, we rushed to our barracks, washed and cleaned our boots, and lined up for our dinner of ersatz coffee, a thin slice of bread, and a tiny square of margarine. We had to eat very fast and get back outside to line up for *appel*. Standing in that line after so many hours of hard work was a terrible punishment. I had to imagine that I was a tree with deep roots in the ground, and this was the anchor that kept me upright. Some men fainted from standing so long. If they fell, they were beaten and forced back into a standing position. If they could not stand, the prisoners on either side of them had to hold them up until the count was complete.

When everyone had been accounted for, we were dismissed. That first night, I went to the small infirmary to get some bandages for my blisters. A doctor put some iodine on my wounds and gave me a roll of paper bandages. I was worried that I wouldn't be able to work with my injured hand the next day. The wounds did take a while to heal, but eventually my hands became as hard as leather.

At approximately 9:30 p.m., a gong sounded, indicating that everyone had to be in his bunk. This was called Lagersperre, and it meant that the camp was closed for the night. Anyone found outside after this could be shot from the guard towers or brought down by a sergeant who was known as Kaduk (Polish for "the Hangman"). Kaduk stalked the streets of the camp with his big German shepherd, which would rip any unfortunate person apart on command.

Once we were in our bunks, the lights were turned off. There was snoring and groaning from the day's hard labour. When we went to sleep, we only took off our boots. I used mine as a pillow, tying the shoelaces to my wrist so people would not be able to steal them from me in the night. As I lay in my bunk, I tried to digest the events of the past twenty-four hours. I thought of my clean and comfortable bed at home, which now seemed a million miles away, and I wondered what the next day had in store.

* * *

After we finished harvesting the mustard, our unit was split in two. We were down to fifty people from the original hundred. My father, my uncle, and I stayed together in the Landwirtschaft Kommando and would be given a new assignment. After one week in Auschwitz, I had learned some of the ropes and was beginning to understand how to exist in this horrible place. But the dreariness of following the same routine every day was draining, and there was no mental stimulation of any kind.

Much worse than the everyday indignities and deprivations were the horrors I was exposed to on a daily basis. I recall coming back to camp from work on the third or fourth day and seeing a body hanging from the gallows, right in our faces. The man wore a sign that read, "This is what happens to people who try to run away from here." It was a shock to see the man hanging, and it was also a warning to keep us in line.

Every day there was another unexpected horror. Those who tried to smuggle in so-called contraband from work—a potato or a beet, for example—were often discovered at the gate, and were given twenty-five lashes for their transgression. This punishment was always meted out at *appel* in the evening, when all inmates were present and had to watch. The accused person was stripped naked and bent over a wooden drum, and his hands and feet were tied down. His back and buttocks were exposed, and he was whipped by a Kapo. In reality, this beating was usually a death sentence, because hardly anyone was able to recover from it. The gallows was located in the same place.

When it was not used to torture and execute inmates, this open square in front of the camp kitchen served other purposes. Sometimes, there was a black market where we could barter our bread rations for rags or something we called *mahorka* (a tobacco made from tree bark). Many of the old-timers were able to get a hold of luxuries such as meat, brandy, cigarettes, cigars, and woollen blankets from Holland. These special items were available only to the Prominente, the prisoners at the very top of the camp hierarchy. The Prominente lived in comfort compared to the rest of us, enjoying separate rooms and special privileges that gave them status and safety. Most importantly, they had connections they could use to procure food, clothing, and other luxuries. The rest of us had absolutely no chance to partake in these exclusive items. In the twisted logic of Auschwitz, this main square was both a place of everyday commerce and bureaucracy, and a site of torture.

CHAPTER 10

Draining Swamps

I t took about a week to harvest all the mustard (although it felt like an eternity), and after that we returned to Budy to pick up our tools for the next assignment. Shovels and hoes were loaded on a two-wheeled cart and brought to a large swampy area, where we were split into two groups. The first group was forced to dig trenches on the edge of the swamp, while the other group, which included me, waded in with boots on to dig channels to direct the water into the perimeter ditch. The sun was burning hot, and my boots and trousers were soon wet and full of mud. Despite all the water around us, we weren't able to drink it because it could cause dysentery, which was often fatal. I had thought the mustard fields were awful, but this was much, much worse.

During our lunch break, my father, my uncle, and I sat together as a family, just as we did every day. The Kapo, Heinrich, must have noticed this, though, because he stood right in front of us and asked my father to identify the person next to him, pointing to my uncle. My father said it was his brother. Then he pointed at me and asked who I was. My father said I was his son. I feared that this was not going to end well.

I had taken my boots off during lunch to try to get the mud out of them, and so I was barefoot when the Kapo yelled at us to get our hoes and get back to work. I rushed to get my boots on while still sitting on the ground, but I wasn't quick enough for Heinrich, who expected his orders to be followed immediately. He began to beat me with his truncheon. I thought my bones were going to crack, but I didn't utter a sound. I had noticed that when the Kapo was beating others, he would pile it on even harder if they yelled out from the pain or begged him to stop. I kept my mouth shut, hoping that he would be more quickly satisfied and would leave me alone. When he was finished with the beating, I grabbed my tools and my boots and ran into the swamp to continue working. This was the first serious beating I'd received in Auschwitz. I was sore and had welts all over my body, but thankfully nothing was broken. Still, I felt violated and humiliated.

The next day, Heinrich went after my father, giving him his own terrible beating. When I saw his pain, I was frustrated that I could do nothing to help him. Later that day, when we returned to camp, my father suggested that we split up, so as not to present an obvious family group. He believed that the Kapo was attacking us because he feared our family unit would strengthen the ties between us. My father thought that if we didn't split up, we would not be able to survive the daily beatings.

Two days later, my father and uncle managed to get into another work unit; I remained with Kapo Heinrich. I don't know how my father and uncle managed to change work units, but it meant that they were moved to a different barracks. For me, this

94

was the start of a new chapter. At fifteen and a half, I was completely on my own during the day, and I had only a few hours to spend with my father and Uncle Eugene before evening lockdown. I was worried about how I would manage without my two guardians, but I was determined to show my father that I had the wherewithal to survive on my own.

After a few days of working in the swamps, my feet were bearing the brunt of the labour. Standing in water all day made my boots soggy, and I couldn't remove them until I got back into my bunk. By the morning, when the boots had dried, it was very difficult to get my feet back into them. I had to force them, and I could no longer use the piece of rag that I had previously wrapped around my feet in place of socks. My heels rubbed against the boots and soon became a bloody mess. With constantly bleeding heels, I had trouble walking. I didn't know how to deal with this problem, which was very worrying because without your feet, you were in big trouble. Every morning, I woke up and focused on making it through the day. My father had always told me to put one foot in front of the other, and this was the advice I repeated to myself constantly.

After a while my heels miraculously healed and I was able to wrap them with a piece of cloth to protect them. In the camp, you had to be inventive and use your smarts to survive. I didn't want my father to worry, so I never told him about my injured feet. And soon I had another concern: by the end of June, I was covered with painful boils from lack of vitamins. My body was screaming for protein, but there was none to be had. My bodily functions were also changing—something I'd observed in many older inmates, who simply could not control their bladders. I began to have the same problems, and soon I found myself climbing down from the top bunk in the middle of the night to rush to the washroom. When we'd first arrived in the camp, my father had said that we should take the top bunks even though it would be harder to get into them as our bodies got weaker. I realized now that being up top at least shielded us from the accidents of those who couldn't make it to the washroom.

Food was the foremost item on our agenda. We thought about it during the day and dreamt about it during the night. I constantly fantasized about meals I'd had at home. I remembered how much I'd hated my mother's tomato soup with rice, but now I thought how wonderful it would be to have a bowl. I told G-d that if I survived and got out of this place, I would be a very good person. I would live happily in a forest alone, and a piece of bread, a potato, and a glass of milk would be a dream come true.

The nights were the time when memories of home and family came flooding back to my mind. How long had it been since I'd left? It was only a couple of months, but it seemed like a thousand years. I could see my family, the faces of each one of them. I didn't want to forget what they looked like or what they had taught me. But at the same time, I knew that if I let my thoughts get too carried away, I would become very vulnerable. So I made myself stop remembering and then was able to sleep more soundly. Still, it always seemed that mornings came much too early, and the Kapo's harsh voice screaming at us to get down from our bunks was a most unwelcome greeting to a new day.

As the days dragged on, I noticed some men with glazed eyes, acting like drunken people who could no longer follow orders. They were beaten, but it made no difference. They had simply given up on living. Inevitably, these men were singled out and taken to the gas chambers. I didn't know about depression at my age, so I worried that the behaviour of these men was somehow contagious. I resolved not to be stricken with what ailed them. There were many times that I faced desperate situations in the weeks and months that followed, but I was determined to survive.

CHAPTER 11

Walking Ghosts

Sometime in June, our unit was marched to Auschwitz II, where the perimeter fence was being enlarged. It was our job to place the many cement pylons to which the electrified fence wires were connected. It took three inmates to lift one of these pylons, which were enormously heavy. It was crushing work that burdened my entire body, especially my shoulders. Each time we were ready to move a pylon, we counted to three and then lifted in unison. We carried the pylon down into a ditch and then up the other side, and placed it into a pre-dug posthole. If one of us faltered or stumbled, we would all have been crushed by its weight. All the while, the Kapo in charge kept harassing us and shouting, "Faster! Faster!"

By the time we'd placed the first pylon, my body was already depleted, and I wondered how I could possibly lift the next one. It took superhuman effort and concentration just to put one foot in front of the other while this crushing weight threatened to push me to the ground. We were assigned to this job for three consecutive days under the strict surveillance of the Kapo, who watched us for any sign of slack or sabotage. My body screamed for water, nourishment, and rest. When our thirty-minute lunch break came, I savoured every drop of the watery soup and each moment of shade under a birch tree.

While having lunch, I noticed a little curl of smoke rising out of the massive chimney of the crematorium. At first it looked quite harmless, but within minutes it was belching out red, angry flames. On humid days, the smoke would not rise but instead stayed low to cover a large area, and ashes rained down in flakes. The odour of burning flesh settled in my nostrils and made me feel sick. By this time, I was quite familiar with the extermination process. I'd heard stories around camp about the gas chambers, and I knew that the Nazis convinced people to enter by telling them that they were going to shower and be disinfected, creating a false sense of security. Once inside, these people—often two thousand at a time—were put to death with Zyklon B gas. Now, as I watched the smoke leave the chimney, I wondered who was in there and where they'd come from.

One day in late June or the beginning of July, we were marched out to work to the sound of the orchestra and I wondered what surprises were in store for me. It was pouring rain. I was soaked and the water ran down my body into my boots. It was a hot and muggy day, so the rain felt good and we were able to drink it to keep ourselves hydrated. I took off my soaked cap, twisted it, and drank the water I was able to wring from it.

We returned again to the satellite camp, Budy, and I saw that the flat cart was piled with woven straw baskets for some unknown purpose. We were led back to the swamps that we had drained of water a few weeks before. Now the fields were somewhat dry, and there was a mountain of white powder at one side.

This chalky substance was the chemical lime (calcium hydroxide), which was used as a fertilizer. We were ordered to load it into the baskets, which quickly became quite heavy because the lime was saturated with rainwater. As soon as we had a full basket, we were directed to the fields we'd drained just a few weeks earlier and were told to apply the lime to the ground. I held the basket on my thigh with my left hand and used my right to scoop out as much as I could to scatter across the field. When the baskets were empty, we walked back and filled them up again. This process went on for many days. The chemical bleached the colour out of our uniforms, and we became known as the Ghost Kommandos.

As the wet lime leached out of the baskets, it went through our jackets and onto our skin. I wanted to scratch my body all over, but that only made it worse—the skin became more irritated, and would crack and bleed. I wondered how I was going to survive this job, but there was no relief. The work detail continued for about a week, until we finished the spreading. By then, the flesh of the fingers on my right hand was eaten away and the skin on my kneecaps was gone, exposing the bone below. I was terrified of being eaten up by this chemical. At the end of each day, I tried to wash it out of my pores, but we had no ointments or treatments to help the skin heal. This was a job that would normally have been done using some sort of equipment, to avoid direct contact with the chemical; however, our health and safety meant nothing to the Nazis. We were expendable.

For the final three days of this detail, we worked near some duck ponds. I could see and hear the ducks as we laboured. At the end of each of the three days, as a form of sport, the Kommandant ordered us to run into the water with our clothes and boots on, and then he told the guards to release their dogs. Those who couldn't run fast enough were mauled. I was aware that when I hit the water, others would pile on top of me and I could be drowned, so I would always try to outrun the others. On the last day, after jumping into the water, I swam into nearby reeds and found a nest with two large duck eggs. It was a miracle. I knew that eating the eggs was dangerous—if someone saw me, I could be harshly disciplined or killed. But they were such a temptation that I didn't care about the consequences. I immediately cracked one open and sucked it out. It tasted wonderful and gave me an infusion of strength that my body so badly needed. When I heard the order to get out of the water and line up for counting, I grabbed the second egg and tucked it into my armpit. I was determined to bring it back to camp for my father. But during the march back, the egg broke. I was devastated to lose this gift that I had so wanted to share. Not so long before, losing a single egg would have seemed like nothing to me, but now this loss was almost impossible to bear.

CHAPTER 12

A Piece of Bacon

One day after coming back from work, I saw my father and my uncle waiting for me inside the gate, just as they always did. My unit was always the last to get back in the evening, and they never failed to wait for my return. A few times, they had managed to bring back a piece of bread or a potato from a work detail, and they always shared their good fortune with me. The risk of doing this was great. As the prisoners came marching back to camp, the SS sergeant in charge of the gate scrutinized each one in search of contraband. If he saw any suspicious behaviour, he would yell to the prisoner to lift up his hands. If the man had anything hidden under his armpit, it would immediately fall out. The sergeant would take offenders out of the column and record their tattoo and barracks numbers. At *appel*, the punishment would be meted out: sometimes lashes from a whip, and sometimes reassignment to a penal unit (Strafkommando). Inmates in penal units were subjected to severe beatings from the Kapos and their lifespans were greatly reduced. In spite of these dangers, prisoners who managed to find scraps of food would always take the risk of trying to smuggle them into the camp. We were constantly on the lookout for items that might improve our chances of survival.

All the belongings of the newly arriving deportees were collected at the rail platform in Auschwitz II–Birkenau and sent for sorting at a special building that came to be known as Kanada. Meats and other food items also ended up in Kanada, where inmate workers sorted through them. Sometimes food items were used to hide valuables—a coin might be hidden in a bread roll, for example. Inmates were allowed to eat the food but were forbidden to take any currency, gold, or jewellery. All valuable items were collected by an SS guard called the Bookkeeper.* On this particular day, my father's unit was working near the Kanada building when a girl from our town recognized him. Having liberal access to food supplies in the luggage, she was able to find a chunk of bacon and managed to slip it to him wrapped in a rag. It was a totally unexpected act of kindness. My father, at great personal risk, smuggled the bacon into Auschwitz I under his jacket, then slipped it to me while we were standing in a huddle. My uncle blocked the view so that nobody would see this transfer. I was surprised to find myself holding a piece of bacon in my hand. We were a traditional Orthodox family, so we did not eat pork of any kind. And yet my father told me that I must eat a little piece of it every day. He and Uncle Eugene, who must have been just as hungry as I, would not break with their religious beliefs, and I marvelled at their strength. But my father told me that this was a matter of life and death, and I must choose life.

---

* In 2015, in perhaps one of the last major Nazi war criminal trials, the "Bookkeeper" Oskar Groening was brought to trial (see epilogue, pages 238–239).

As slave labourers, we had no lockers to store things, but I had managed to dislodge one of the ceiling tiles above my bunk in the barracks, creating a small space where I hid a few odds and ends, including pieces of rag. I stashed the bacon in the space behind this tile. For the next several nights, I waited until every-one was asleep and then, when I was certain that nobody could observe me, dislodged the tile and pulled out my secret treasure. Without a knife or any other utensils, I chewed off a small piece of the bacon. I could actually feel the energy flowing into my body from this sustenance. Every night, I had another bite—just a small shot of energy—and I am positive that this little bit of protein gave me the strength I needed to face the next day.

CHAPTER 13

Selections, July 1944

The SS initiated a wave of selections in Auschwitz I in early July 1944. Simply hearing the word *selection* sent fear through me. My fellow prisoners had explained the entire gassing and cremation process to me, and I knew that selection meant certain death. I made a firm decision that if I was selected, I would try to electrocute myself on the fences or get shot from the guard towers, rather than submit to being gassed.

One night, we were abruptly awakened from our sleep. SS guards and Kapos were yelling, "*Raus!* Selection! Leave your clothes in your bunk and get down to the ground floor." They herded us onto the street between the barracks and forced us to run to a nearby building where SS doctors were waiting to make the selection. We filed by them in a single line. They looked at each inmate to determine who was too weak or sick to work and who could continue. I knew that my life was hanging in the balance, and the fear almost froze me at a point when I should have looked most alive and capable of physical labour. The person in front of me was stopped, and his tattoo and barracks numbers were recorded on a clipboard. This was a death sentence for him but an opportunity to live for me. While he was stopped, I simply kept moving toward the exit of the building, breathing a sigh of relief when I got there. I knew that if I had paused for even a moment, they might have scrutinized me more closely and sent me to my death. I was lucky this time.

Back in the barracks, I couldn't get to sleep. I wondered what had happened to my father and my uncle, who were in a different barracks than I was. How did they fare? I would have to wait until the morning to find out.

The next day, I ran to their barracks, but they were not there. I thought the worst must have happened. I had no time to investigate further, however, because I had to join my unit for *appel*. I spent a horrendously difficult day thinking about them, but I tried to convince myself that they had just been selected to join another work camp. I hoped for the best, but inside I knew that I was lying to myself.

When I returned from my work that evening, I went immediately to their barracks again. Still they were not there. I asked people in the bunks next to theirs if they had seen them, but no one had. I ran to a fenced-off holding area where the SS kept the selected prisoners until they were ready to transport them to Birkenau to be gassed. I saw many people milling around inside this area, and I called the names of my father and uncle. Within seconds, they came to meet me at the barbed-wire fence. I was so happy to see them, but at the same time, I knew these were likely our last moments together. I didn't have any words. I couldn't express a single word of consolation or hope. The guard from the tower yelled, "Move away from the fence immediately or I will shoot!" My father reached out across the wire and blessed me with a classic Jewish prayer: "May G-d bless you and safeguard you. May He be gracious unto you. May He turn His countenance to you and give you peace." This was the same prayer my father once uttered to bless his children every Friday evening before the Sabbath meal. Then he said, "If you survive, you must tell the world what happened here. Now go." As I walked away, I took one final look before I turned the corner of the building and was unable to see them any longer.*

I was devastated and confused. How does a father feel when he is saying goodbye and leaving his son in such an evil place? For days, I barely existed, drifting along in a constant haze. My two guardian angels were gone. Without their encouragement and their small gifts of food, I never would have survived the first two weeks in Auschwitz. Now I was the only living member of my immediate family—a sad, lonely, and daunting feeling. How was I going to survive without them?

* See appendix.

Chapter 14

Land Reclamation Outside Auschwitz

O ne day, the SS marched us to a large tract of land that was overgrown with scrub and full of large tree stumps. We were directed to clear the entire area and level the soil because they wanted to use the land for growing grain and mustard. Although the hot sun beat down on us, the fresh air was invigorating and it didn't seem that this work would be as rigorous as our former jobs. We had space to move around and we could use the bushes as a sort of a camouflage so we were not under the constant surveillance of the Kapo or the Kommandant. The guards and their attack dogs were spread out along the perimeter of the work area, and while I could not see them, I knew they were constantly patrolling in a circle. I thought of trying to escape, but I soon realized that there was no chance of success. Being under constant watch was like having a ball and chain around my neck. The Kapo drove us mercilessly to work at a fast pace, but we had some respite because he had such a large zone to patrol.

The SS divided us into units to perform different tasks, such as cutting bushes and hauling the branches to an area designated for burning. Others levelled the land or filled ditches with soil. My unit of four was ordered to dig out the roots of the large stumps. Two of us had pickaxes to loosen the soil and two of us had shovels to remove it. We were to dig in a circle around the stumps so that the roots could be exposed and severed, and then remove the stumps. I estimated that we would be doing this work for about one week.

Around noon each day, a horse-drawn cart brought canisters of watery soup and we had thirty minutes of rest. Lunch was always a risky time because of the jostling and shoving for position. Your spot in the lineup often determined how thick, and therefore how filling, your meal was. We were like ravenous wolves desperate for sustenance. If a prisoner was in the good graces of the person ladling the soup, he had a chance to get more of the vegetables that settled at the bottom of the canister. I told myself that if I survived, I would never, ever stand in line for anything again. I felt that there was no humanity here, only degradation, dehumanization, and the desire to grind us away, body and soul. We were forced to fight over soup so that we could go on.

One day while I was savouring my watery soup, I heard the whistle of a locomotive a short distance away. We were on a plateau near a river and some railway tracks, and I was eager to see what was coming our way. When the locomotive drew near, I could see that it was pulling many flat cars. Each flat car carried two big tanks, and on each tank there were soldiers in black SS overalls. They were singing, laughing, and waving as they went by. My thoughts turned inward, and I wished that I were free to sing and laugh as they did. I had not laughed once since my arrival in this harsh world two months earlier. But then I realized that these soldiers were going east to face the tank units of the Russian Red Army, and I wondered if they'd be laughing then.

After eating our soup, we continued to dig until the Kapo told us to assemble and be counted for the march back to the camp. I was tired, thirsty, and in need of sustenance. I was looking forward to the evening cup of ersatz coffee, a thin slice of bread, and a tiny square of margarine, as well as being able to rest on my wooden bunk.

By now, we were a seasoned marching unit, with the Kapo calling out the orders and setting the pace. We sang German marching songs as we went. The marching and singing helped me feel more normal, and empowered me to go on from day to day in this distressful situation. It also showed our guards that we could not be beaten down; in fact, they had to hustle to keep up with our pace. If the wind was blowing in our direction, I could hear the sound of the camp orchestra as we neared. More and more, this music was an integral part of my camp life. Like the coffee and the bit of bread, it sustained me.

The next day, we were working in a deep cavity we'd dug; all the excavated soil formed a mound that hid us from view. This gave us a feeling of security, and we let down our guard. It was a dangerous mistake, because the mound also prevented us from seeing if anyone was approaching. At one point, we were loafing carelessly, holding our tools in our hands, when suddenly two of my co-workers jumped up and furiously started to work again. I felt a blow on the back of my head. Although I did not feel any pain, there was a buzz in my ears and a feeling of dizziness overcame me. When I tried to pick up my shovel to resume working, I felt something warm dripping down my neck and I saw blood. I turned around to see an SS guard standing behind me, and I realized that I had received a blow from the butt of his gun. Our eyes locked for a second and I saw his twisted, evil grimace. I thought I was looking at the devil.

Blood continued to pour from the wound, and I went into shock and collapsed. The other prisoners hauled me out of the pit and threw me into a nearby ditch to keep me out of the way until the end of the day. The blood continued to ooze out of the wound, and eventually the under-Kapo, a man named Stasek, approached. He tore off a piece of my prisoner garb and told me to urinate on it and then put it on the back of my head. This bandage eventually stopped the bleeding, and I was thankful to him. Without his assistance and advice, I would not have made it back to camp.

I was no longer able to participate in the work detail. I tried, but my feet would not cooperate and my legs couldn't hold me up. My thoughts ran on like a movie, a retrospective of my life up until that moment. I recalled my father's parting words—about telling the world what happened at Auschwitz—and I knew I would not be able to fulfil his final wish. My demise would be the end of the family Eisen.

When it came time for lunch, I watched from the ditch as the soup was ladled out, but I could not go there and no one would bring any to me. I was simply written off. At some point, Kommandant Kuntz probably received a report that our unit was down one prisoner, and he came to have a look at me. I thought he would pull his pistol from his holster and shoot me on the spot. Instead, he signalled with his right hand, his finger pointing up in a circular motion, meaning that I was going to go up the chimney of the crematorium. I understood that my fate was sealed. A feeling of helplessness and fright overtook me. How could I prepare myself to face the gas chamber? I would be reduced to a simple pile of ashes. I had always planned, as a last resort, to run to the electrified fence and die by my own action, but this was no longer an option because I had lost my mobility. I began to wish that the Kommandant had put a bullet in my head. I thought of my family and how they must have felt while facing their own demise. When my mother entered the gas chamber, she had my three siblings in her care. How she must have fought until the last breath in that horrible chamber. What would it be like for me? Slow or fast? Would my soul leave my body? Would I meet my family again? Would they all be waiting for me? How would I know them? What shape or form would they be in? I felt utterly alone, with no one to take care of or comfort me. No one could save me.

At the end of the day, our work unit was lined up and counted. All the tools were loaded on the two-wheeled cart, and I was thrown on top. As the unit proceeded to march back to camp, I was acutely aware of what I saw and heard around me; it was the last time I would experience any of it. The cart was left in a shed with all the tools in it, and two inmates took hold of my arms and dragged me a short distance through the gates of the camp. Under-Kapo Stasek directed them to the hospital in barrack 21, where I was left in a hallway, near the surgery room.

CHAPTER 15

The Operating Room

I was carried into the operating room and my bloody jacket, pants, and boots were removed. I was placed on an operating table, and someone put a mask on my face and administered ether. When I awoke, I found myself in a bed with the taste of anaesthetic in my mouth. My head was bandaged, and I was groggy and weak. I was surprised that I was still alive after the traumatic experience of the previous day. Looking at my surroundings, I saw patients who were sickly and skeletal. Instinct told me that I needed to leave this place as soon as possible. Although I was dizzy and weak, I managed to get out of bed on my own. I was determined to walk around the ward by holding on to the bed frames. Eventually, I had to lie back down to gain strength.

There were two doctors in charge of this ward: Dr. Jakob Gordon, a Polish Jew, and a French Jew named Dr. Samuel Steinberg. At mid-morning, the chief surgeon, a Polish political prisoner named Dr. Tadeusz Orzeszko, came into the room to check on the patients who were recovering from operations.

A photo of Dr. Tadeusz Orzeszko, taken on his incarceration at Auschwitz I,
July 29, 1943.

When it was my turn to be examined, Dr. Gordon removed the paper bandages and the chief surgeon inspected the wound on the back of my head. Satisfied, Dr. Orzeszko instructed Dr. Gordon to put on new bandages.

To my surprise, I found my boots placed carefully under my bed. But I wore a straggly surgical gown and had no other clothes. When I asked Dr. Gordon if he could get me some coverings, he obliged by giving me a pair of white cotton pants and a white shirt. These were the clothes worn by the doctors under their white coats. I felt clean and presentable for the first time in months. The daily rations were the same, but I was given a watery Cream of Wheat–type cereal, which was reserved for hospital patients. When this cereal got cold, it became rubbery and I could hardly swallow it.

All patients still in the ward after three days were deemed unfit for work and taken to the gas chambers. On the morning of my third day in the ward, the SS sergeant in charge of barrack 21 arrived with stretcher-bearers and began to collect the tags of the patients to be removed. As each patient was laid on the stretcher, his identity card was placed beside him. When my turn came, I feared I was in great danger. The stretcher-bearers carried us down the stairs to the main hallway; from there, we were to be taken out the door and loaded onto waiting trucks.

The chief surgeon, Dr. Orzeszko, was standing in the main hallway when we appeared. He was a tall, well-muscled man, with short blond hair and steel-blue eyes. He had an aura of calm confidence about him. When he saw me, he stopped the stretcher-bearers, helped me get up, and took my identification tag. He then led me to the prep room of the surgery, where he gave me a lab coat and told me that I would now do the cleaning and other duties required for the efficient running of the operating theatre.

Prior to my recruitment, this job was filled by a young Polish medical student who was serving a one-year sentence as a political prisoner. He was due to be released in about three days, and I would be his replacement. The student trained me during his remaining days on the job, and I keenly observed him and learned the importance of running the unit smoothly and efficiently. There was a long list of things to do. I had confidence in my cleaning abilities because of my apprentice work with the furrier, but it was intimidating to see medical instruments and other equipment that I had no idea how to use. I was determined to succeed, however, and I knew my life depended on my performance.

The prep room had two sinks with hot and cold water where the surgeons washed before surgery. There was a huge autoclave for sterilizing sheets, gowns, masks, gloves, and other items, and a sterilizer for instruments with several trays and a timer that had to be set. I had to learn these and many other duties. The shelves in the credenzas were neatly laid out with instruments such as clamps, scalpels, hammers, saws, chisels, scissors of all shapes and sizes, syringes, and needles. There were two worktables to prepare items and compounds before surgeries. The storage cabinets were filled with supplies such as paper bandages, cotton balls, gypsum for casts, cleaning supplies, disinfectants, brooms and mops, buckets, and other odds and ends. The surgery itself had a basic operating table with an overhead light, several portable floodlights, and a credenza in which Novocain and ether were stored. We did not have blood plasma or intravenous therapy.

At first, I was not comfortable watching the surgeons perform, particularly when I saw them make the opening incision. But I quickly became used to the sight of blood and the gore of the operating room. When the surgeons finished their job, they came out through the swinging door into the prep room and removed their gowns and gloves. Two orderlies would arrive, put the patient on a gurney, and take him to the upstairs ward. It was my job to immediately mop the floor and clean and disinfect the operating table. I had to be quick about it. Within thirty minutes, another patient would be laid out on the table and made ready for his operation. I had all the responsibility for the efficient upkeep of these two rooms so that the doctors could continue to perform their tasks.

Every night, patients awaiting surgery the next day had to receive enemas. My duty was to administer the enema and help the patients evacuate their bowels. I did not like this task in the beginning, but it became routine and necessary. If the patient didn't have an enema, he could soil the operating table and the post-surgery cleanup would be twice as difficult.

Day after day, new patients arrived at barrack 21. They were skeletal, weak, and sickly, and near the end of their struggles. They also knew that unless they could walk out of that ward on their own two feet, their next stop was the gas chamber. So every patient faced a bleak dilemma. Many had severe hernias, phlegmon (flesh-eating disease), broken limbs, burst appendices, or severe injuries from bullets that tore the flesh and destroyed bones. Watching them stoically accept their fate inside the twisted logic of the concentration camp made me realize how brave they were.

The surgeons at barrack 21 did their very best under impossible conditions. The surgery ward was, in many respects, a ruse to show how "well" the Nazis looked after their inmates. These patients were destined for annihilation, because in most cases they were beyond help. But the surgeons still took their job seriously and did the best they could for their patients. The doctors were themselves prisoners, and they had to dance to the tune of the SS officers in charge of the camp. My job, in the scheme of things, was simply to make sure that the operating room was shiny and clean at all times.

My workday started at 7 a.m. and usually lasted for twelve hours. My system was strict and precise. I started my day by sprinkling talcum powder on the floor of the prep room and the surgery, and then standing on two rags and using my feet in a polishing motion until the linoleum shone. I picked up the freshly washed linens, gowns, and masks from the laundry barracks and packed them neatly into three perforated drums. Next, I loaded the drums into the autoclave, closed and bolted the lid, and turned on the high-pressure steam so that the linens were sterilized. Finally, I prepared the instruments for that day's operations. When the surgeons arrived at 10 a.m., I had the water boiled for their tea and I took a fifteen-minute break before the first operation began. The patients were lined up on a bench in the hallway, and I called their numbers in the order that was given to me. While the surgeons were washing up, I helped the patient onto the table and covered him with a sheet, and then I went to the prep room to help the surgeons tie their gowns and masks and to hold the latex gloves so they could put their hands into them. Patients who were being operated on from the waist down were given a spinal needle with Novocain by the doctors. Sometimes I had to administer ether to those who were being operated on above the waist, and I instructed them to count backwards from thirty to one as the ether took effect. My final task was to bring the instruments to the operating table and lay them out before the assistant surgeon.

After the last operation of the day, the surgeons left and I was charged with putting the rooms in order again for the next day. I realized quite early on that I had to have an efficient system so that no time would be wasted and the work would flow easily. At the end of the day, my job involved gathering all the bloody sheets, gowns, towels, and masks and delivering them to the laundry barracks next door for cleaning. This laundry was open twenty-four hours a day, disinfecting clothing for thousands of inmates. I got to know the Kapo in charge, and one day I dared to ask him for a clean jacket and pants. He took me to a pile of clothes and let me pick garments that fit me better than what I had on. I also managed to get clean material for dusting and cleaning the operating theatre and prep room, and some material to wrap around my feet for socks. He was an important contact. I was not in the upper strata of the camp hierarchy, but working in the hospital did give me some small privileges. In the camp, we used the word *organizuj* to mean ways to improve our lot or survive the debilitating hunger. If you found an extra resource that could be bartered for shoes, food, or clothing, it could make the difference between life and death.

My next task after the laundry was to sweep and mop the operating room floors—and the walls, if necessary. Then I had to wash all the instruments, especially the clamps, which had to be brushed carefully to eliminate any tissue on them; the scissors, syringes, scalpels, and needles I kept separately to avoid cuts to my fingers. When they were clean, I laid them out to dry; all the moisture had to be removed before they were placed into the credenzas in an organized fashion. The scalpels also had to be sharpened on a fine stone and made ready for use.

When the prep room and operating room were clean and ready for the next day, I put out the lights and went upstairs to my bunk in a room I shared with the doctors and the orderlies. I was dead tired at the end of every day, but it always took me a while to fall asleep. I realized how lucky I was to be working in barrack 21 in spite of my devastating head injury, which had actually turned out to be my lucky break.

CHAPTER 16

Surgeries in Barrack 21

One afternoon, I saw a female patient brought in by ambulance from Auschwitz II–Birkenau, supposedly for an operation to repair a burst appendix. Dr. Orzeszko reached into a closed cabinet and retrieved a special instrument with a long stem and an oval-shaped scraper at the end. I had not seen this type of instrument in use before. The patient was a healthy-looking woman and her head was not shaved like those of the other female inmates. While I sterilized the instruments, I heard the doctor speak with her in Polish and I guessed that she was a more prominent inmate. Before the operation began, several Polish political prisoners, barracks elders, and room elders arrived in the prep room and huddled with Dr. Orzeszko. From the little Polish that I understood, I gathered that they were going to position themselves all the way to the main gate and warn us if there were any SS officers heading toward the surgery.

I watched as Dr. Orzeszko made the initial incision for an appendix operation and then simply tied up the veins and immediately stitched up the wound. Was this some kind of surface operation? I was confused, but it was not for me to ask questions. I was instructed to fetch an empty pail, and when I came back, I found the patient strapped into leg holders. Dr. Orzeszko told me to crouch under the operating table, holding the pail while he inserted the long instrument into the patient's vagina. Blood started to flow into the pail within minutes, and I saw the tiny head, arms, and legs of a fetus. The doctor told me to immediately flush the pail's contents away, and to make sure that no one saw me do it. When I came back to the operating room, I unstrapped the patient's legs and cleaned her body of blood; the orderlies put her on a stretcher and loaded her into the ambulance, and she was gone. This was the only time I saw a female patient attended to.

I was tense throughout the operation, and I understood how dangerous a situation it was. When the woman was safely on her way back to Auschwitz II–Birkenau, I sensed that the two surgeons breathed a sigh of relief—more, I assumed, because they had not been caught with her, and not so much because the procedure was a success. This type of cooperation was possible because the Polish political prisoners were in a different category than Jews and others. Any Jewish woman who was found to be pregnant was immediately put to death, because the Nazi racial ideology was founded on the eradication of all Jewish children. But pregnancy was also a risk for Polish prisoners. The Polish inmates had a sophisticated underground resistance that operated right under the noses of the Nazis, and because of that, they were able to help each other in critical situations. Had the camp administrators found out about the abortion, I'm sure that we would all have been done for.

* * *

On another occasion, a patient was brought to barrack 21 accompanied by two Gestapo men. They arrived after the day's surgeries had ended and I was cleaning up. They instructed me to summon the two surgeons to the operating room immediately. When Dr. Orzeszko arrived in the prep room, they gave him an envelope with X-ray films. The patient was around sixty years old, and he was infected with tuberculosis in two of his ribs just above his heart. He was distinguished and well dressed, with longer hair and a beautiful tweed jacket. Dr. Orzeszko spoke to him in German about his symptoms, and I detected a Hungarian accent in his speech. It appeared that he was doing important work for the Nazi regime.

I helped the man undress and get onto the table, and I covered him with a sheet. Dr. Orzeszko told me to fetch and sterilize certain instruments, including a stainless-steel handsaw and cutting pliers. I sensed that this was going to be a difficult operation. Dr. Orzeszko and his assistant surgeon discussed the procedure they were going to follow: they would cut a four-inch length of bone from the two diseased ribs near the heart. They seemed concerned about how they could perform this operation with such limited instruments and resources, but they nevertheless got ready to proceed. I had to shave the patient's left chest area, then he was put to sleep and the operation began.

After the first incision, the veins were clamped and the two ribs were exposed. Dr. Orzeszko sawed the man's ribs carefully, aware of the risks with the heart so near. After a long day of operating, he must have been very tired and I had to continually wipe his forehead of sweat. Eventually, the diseased ribs were removed and I could see the heart pumping in the patient's chest. Unfortunately, Dr. Orzeszko could not find one unclamped vein, and it was bleeding profusely. He filled a bucket with bloody gauze and seemed very concerned because the patient's heartbeat was slowing and he was losing a lot of blood. Immediate action had to be taken.

Dr. Orzeszko told me to grab a loaf of bread from the pantry in the prep room, use it to bribe an orderly in the ward upstairs, and bring him down to the operating theatre. This orderly was placed on a gurney next to the operating table, and Dr. Orzeszko rigged up a tube with two needles. One was inserted into a vein in the patient's left hand and the other into a vein the orderly's right hand. A valve to control the blood flow was operated by Dr. Orzeszko's assistant. If the blood flow was not regulated, it could have put the patient into shock. This was a direct body-to-body blood transfusion.

Dr. Orzeszko watched carefully as the patient's heartbeat and colour seemed to stabilize. He also managed to find and clamp the bleeding vein. All of us in the operating room were quite relieved. The veins were tied, the clamps were removed and counted, and the incision was stitched up. We hoped the men's blood types were compatible, but we had no way of knowing. The patient was put back into the ambulance, and he and his entourage left the camp. I marvelled at the quick thinking and stamina of the doctors who performed under these circumstances, and I learned an important lesson about how to act in situations for which you're unprepared, and how to use the resources that are at hand.

* * *

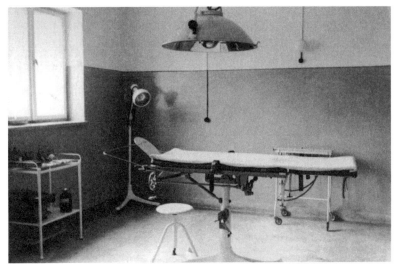

The prep room (above) contained sinks for washing up; an autoclave for sterilizing gowns, linens and other items; a large corner fireplace; a sterilizer for instruments; and a storage cabinet with glass doors. The operating room (below) was austerely equipped with the most basic implements. Photos courtesy of Yad Vashem.

One day, a young man dressed in partisan clothes—riding pants, riding boots, a heavy pullover, and a short winter coat—was brought to the operating room by an ambulance guarded by two Gestapo men. The femur of his right leg was completely shattered and only hanging on by some muscles. The Gestapo agents told Dr. Orzeszko that if he failed to save the man's life, he would forfeit his own.

When we placed the patient on the operating table, it was obvious he had lost a lot of blood. It was a terrible wound. Dr. Orzeszko spoke to the man in Polish while I was in the prep room getting the instruments ready. The assistant surgeon worked on several steel plates, drilling holes and making strips that could be used to join the shattered bones with screws. I placed all these items, together with the instruments, into the sterilization chamber. It was a very difficult operation because Dr. Orzeszko had to remove several inches of bone and join the stumps with the steel plates. He tried to give the patient as much height as possible when joining the bones, but the wounded leg still ended up being two inches shorter than the good one. The patient was in a coma when he was taken to barrack 11 by the Gestapo.

I later learned that, prior to the operation, Dr. Orzeszko had found out the man was a member of the Polish resistance and asked him about the location of his home unit. Knowing that the only reason the Gestapo wanted to save his life was to torture him for information when he recovered, Dr. Orzeszko put him into a medically induced coma to buy enough time to warn the man's unit to disperse or relocate before the Gestapo could extract their whereabouts.

* * *

Phlegmon, a flesh-eating disease, was prevalent among prisoners because of the lack of food and nourishment. On one occasion, we operated on a patient with a severe case that had spread above one knee, meaning the leg had to be amputated. I was instructed to hold the leg while the doctor sawed through the femur to sever it. After the amputation, I found myself holding the diseased leg and wondering what to do with it. Although I had seen countless operations by that point, I had never before been in this situation, and I was quite upset. I placed the leg on the floor of the operating room and watched as the doctors closed the wound on the patient's thigh. A tube was inserted for drainage, and he was removed to the upstairs ward. I got busy cleaning up the room and the instruments, but I avoided attending to the leg on the floor. At last, Dr. Orzeszko told me to take it to the experimental barracks next to the surgery. I had never been to barrack 22 before, but I'd heard that terrible experiments were performed there. I did not want to hear about these experiments, and I certainly did not want to see them. But I had a job to do.

I wrapped the leg in a sheet, put it over my shoulder, and set off for barrack 22. The building emitted a strong smell of formaldehyde. I reported my presence to the SS officer in charge and asked him where to deposit the leg. He led me to a room that had formaldehyde-filled tubs crammed with human body parts of all kinds. When he told me to throw the leg in one, I gingerly lowered it in without the sheet. My whole body shivered from the sights and odours of this barracks, and I couldn't wait to get away.

On my way out, I saw a group of naked young boys huddled together in a room. These boys had been castrated, and I saw surgical thread hanging from their penises; they appeared to be in a state of shock and confusion. I couldn't see in their eyes or demeanour even the tiniest spark of life. I returned hastily to the barracks and continued my work, thankful that I was still whole but unable to forget the look in those boys' eyes.

* * *

In the months of July, August, and September of 1944, American bombers flew overhead at noon almost on a daily basis. They were targeting installations that were producing ammunitions and other war materials, such as the Weichsel-Union-Metallwerke near Auschwitz I and the I.G. Farben synthetic rubber plant at Monowitz (Auschwitz III). A siren alerted the camp population that a bombing raid was imminent, and all units working within a reasonable distance of the camp were to return to ensure that no one could escape during heavy bombing. Once all the work units were inside the camp, the main gate was locked and the high-voltage wires activated to deter any escapees.

A single Pathfinder airplane would fly overhead and drop a flare to mark the place for the bombers to begin releasing their payload. Within minutes, you could hear the drone of the bombers' powerful engines. It was quite a sight. They flew in squadrons, spaced evenly, in a display of force that filled me with hope. Finally it appeared that higher powers were coming and my chain of slavery would be broken. I thought that America was coming to liberate us, and that the Nazis would be made to pay for all the evils they had perpetrated.

As the bombs fell, the ground shook like an earthquake and shrapnel flew through the air. Under my breath, I said, "Keep dropping the bombs." Later I learned that the US Air Force bombed during the day, and the British Royal Air Force bombed throughout the night. The camp's anti-aircraft guns, which were purposely placed near the perimeter fence to ensure their safety, fired on the squadrons of bombers, but the planes were mostly out of range. One airplane was hit and started to spin to earth—an upsetting sight until I saw parachutes open and knew the crew had exited the stricken aircraft. By the summer of 1944, the Allies ruled the skies over occupied Poland, and I never saw a single German fighter plane attack the Allied bombers. I longed to be as free as the pilots above, whose movements were not controlled by evil forces.

Sometime in September, there was a heavy bombing raid while we were in the middle of an operation. We had to stop our work, and I opened the windows in the surgery and the prep room so that the glass would not shatter from the exploding bombs. Outside, shrapnel and shards of glass were landing all over the camp. When the bombers left, the all-clear sirens sounded. I closed the windows and the operation resumed.

While I was preparing for the next patient, the door to the prep room opened and an unfamiliar SS officer began speaking to Dr. Orzeszko. He ordered him to clear the operating room for several injured SS personnel who were en route by ambulance. This officer announced that he would perform the operations, and that Dr. Orzeszko was to assist him. He was Dr. Fischer, the camp doctor, and he was responsible for ensuring that no contagious diseases developed in the camp and endangered SS personnel.

Several stretchers were brought into barrack 21 and lined up in the hallway. Dr. Fischer and Dr. Orzeszko checked the condition of the injured SS men to assess who would be attended to first. Most of them had shrapnel wounds in their legs, chests, and arms. I was instructed to cut off their uniforms and prepare them for surgery. These SS men were bleeding and moaning from pain, and I could see that the colour of their blood was the same as mine. These killers were not so brave when they were laid out flat on their backs. I suddenly felt elated at the thought that a fifteen-year-old Jewish teenager was in charge while they lay there, totally helpless.

Dr. Fischer unbuckled his belt with his sidearm and handed it to me along with his jacket. He then sat on a stool to wash up for the operation, while I controlled the water temperature. He asked me to cover his riding pants with towels so they would not get wet, and then he asked me for my name, my place of origin, and my date of arrival in Auschwitz. He also asked me where my family was, but I didn't dare tell him what had happened to them. I told him I didn't know. I'm not sure why he asked me about my family when he must have known what happened to the Hungarian transports.

When Dr. Fischer had finished washing up, I held up the sterilized gown so he could put his hands inside. He was over six feet tall, so I had to get up on a stool to tie the gown around his waist and neck. I also tied on his mask and held out the latex gloves while he put them on. I placed the instruments in the sterilizer but made an instantaneous decision to disinfect them for only five minutes rather than the required twenty. I had no desire to use safe methods on SS criminals, and I justified my actions by telling myself that I was in a war and this was the only tool I had to fight the enemy. We operated on the SS soldiers for two days in our surgery until the bombed-out SS hospital near Birkenau was back in action.

* * *

In late November 1944, a teenager slipped out of his barracks after the camp was locked down for the night and tried to break into the kitchen facilities. He was intercepted by Sergeant Kaduk, who took great pleasure in torturing and beating people he found outside of their barracks after lockdown. From my bed, I heard Kaduk's dog barking, and shortly after that I heard machine-gun fire from the guard tower. The teenager was shot in the head. He was brought to the surgery right away for an emergency operation. I was summoned to the operating room and the surgeons arrived soon after.

We placed the boy on the operating table, and I could see a severe bullet wound on the left side of his temple with an exit wound at the back of his head. A large part of his skull was shattered, and he was in a coma. The surgeons cleaned the wound, removed bone chips, stopped the bleeding, and stitched him up. There was nothing more they could do for him.

The orderlies took him to the upstairs ward, where Dr. Gordon took charge of him. He was the only critical patient in the ward, and all the doctors took a particular interest in his survival. Many days later, he emerged from his coma and opened his eyes. Dr. Gordon spoke to him, but there was no response. He was paralyzed and we could not give him any sustenance and had no intravenous fluids to sustain him. He was trapped in his body, eyes open, with no way to respond. He appeared to have massive brain damage. Dr. Gordon periodically tested the boy's nerve responses by pricking his hands and feet with a needle, and after a week, he showed some response to the needle on one side of his body. When Dr. Gordon spoke to him, the boy moved his eyes as if he understood. Dr. Gordon worked closely with him, teaching him to speak again. He was kept alive only because it was near the end of the war and the gas chambers had been destroyed by order of the camp Kommandant.

Around the same time, another teenager was brought into the operating room with severe pain in his belly. When the surgeon opened him up, he realized it was a ruptured appendix and the teenager died on the operating table. We all felt sadness at the death of such a young person. His body was taken to the experimental barracks next door for disposal.

Of all my experiences in the prep room, the most shocking task came when the SS men removed patients from the upstairs ward to the Birkenau gas chambers and returned about two hours later with their pockets full of teeth wrapped in bloody rags. I was ordered to remove the gold crowns and fillings from these teeth because I had access to medical instruments. As I worked, I couldn't help thinking that just a short time before, the owners of these teeth had been alive. And now they were just a pile of ash. Removing the gold crowns and fillings traumatized me, and I felt that in some small way, I was participating in the desecration of their remains. I wondered how many SS men enriched themselves by scavenging the remains of their hundreds of thousands of victims.

CHAPTER 17

A Pot of Stew

I t was a well-known fact among the prisoners that unless a door opened for you, it was impossible to get out of Auschwitz alive. My head wound was, ironically, exactly the door that I needed. It had saved me from the rigorous work on the Landwirtschaft Kommando. But even that opportunity would not have been possible without the immediate first aid I received from Under-Kapo Stasek, who stopped the bleeding and arranged for my delivery to the surgery in barrack 21. Without his initiative, my story would have ended in that scrubby field of tree stumps. I also owed my life to Dr. Orzeszko, who not only operated on my wound but also took me off the stretcher before I was sent to the gas chamber in Birkenau.

I worked in the operating room for six months, and my structured daily routines allowed me to survive away from the severe hard labour and the threat of the SS guards and the Kapos. Dr. Orzeszko was a dedicated and skilful surgeon who was respected by his peers and the Polish political prisoners of Auschwitz I. I suspected that he also played an integral role in the Polish underground in the camp, a fact that was later confirmed by his family.

A short while after I started working in the operating room, Dr. Orzeszko opened a pantry door and showed me shelves loaded with food supplies, including loaves of bread, salami, onions, potatoes, carrots, salt and pepper, and a large cooking pot. I was astounded at this bonanza—more food than I'd seen since I left my home in April 1944. He told me how to prepare a stew with all the provisions, and how to use the autoclave as a pressure cooker. I salivated at the scent of the cooking food. Of course, there was always the worry that the aroma would give us away, so this activity was done after all the operations were finished and the SS officer in charge of the barracks had left for the night. The meal was ready in less than an hour, and in no time I felt that my stomach was so full it might burst. I couldn't believe that I'd just had a bowl of goulash in Auschwitz! The leftovers were locked in the pantry and consumed the next day. The ingredients for our stews were sent by the chief cook, and I knew that I was one of the privileged few who had access to such provisions. The extra calories made a huge difference in my overall health and stamina, and this nourishment was key to my survival.

Dr. Orzeszko, like other Polish political prisoners, was allowed to receive small monthly care packages containing food and other supplies. He was also allowed to receive and write one letter per month. When the doctor's package was delivered to the operating room, he would open it with tremendous care, as if wanting to feel the love from his family members back home. I was happy for him, but it only reinforced the fact that Jewish inmates didn't have this same privilege. There was no one left to send us these precious gifts.

CHAPTER 18

The Destruction of Crematorium 4

The Sonderkommandos were Jewish inmates forced to work twelve-hour shifts disposing of the victims of the gas chambers. After each gassing procedure, they removed the bodies from the chambers, cut off the victims' hair, extracted gold crowns from their mouths, and cut open body orifices in search of treasure that might have been ingested or hidden. (Even the hair had economic value, because the Nazis could make it into fabric.) This was the most gruesome and soul-destroying job that any human could endure. And if the work itself wasn't bad enough, the Nazis gassed the Sonderkommandos every sixty days to ensure that there were no witnesses to their crimes, so the men knew their own deaths were imminent.

On October 7, 1944, Crematorium 4 was blown up by the Sonderkommandos. They had fashioned rudimentary explosives from gunpowder, which they'd obtained from women inmates who worked in the Weichsel-Union-Metallwerke factory. They'd also prepared Molotov cocktails. When a unit of SS men came in to oversee their execution, the inmates threw the Molotov cocktails at them, killing several of them, and then blew up the crematorium. In the chaos that followed, the Sonderkommandos broke out through the gate and ran toward the perimeter of the camp. Guards began shooting at them, and large reinforcements of SS units were immediately organized and sent in pursuit. They shot down most of the men. Of the approximately six hundred Sonderkommando inmates involved in the rebellion, only six managed to escape through the three cordons around the camp into the nearby forest.

As a result of this uprising, the inmates of Auschwitz I and Auschwitz II were made to stand at *appel* all night as a form of collective punishment. Many simply dropped and died from exhaustion. As I stood, I was not only exhausted but also extremely fearful of other consequences, and when we were finally dismissed, I was relieved to go back to the operating room to continue my daily duties.

The Nazi officials immediately launched an investigation to determine how the Sonderkommandos had managed to get a hold of the explosive powder. The makeup of the powder was specific to each factory, and the evidence led them to Weichsel-Union-Metallwerke, where hundreds of women from Birkenau were working as slave labourers. Eventually, the Gestapo were able to identify four young women, and these women were brought to barrack 11 at Auschwitz I for interrogation. We heard nothing more until January 5, 1945, when the entire camp was assembled in front of the gallows in Auschwitz l. There were many SS guard units lined up to form a barrier between the inmates and the gallows, and the Lagerkommandant soon arrived with his own personal SS guards to oversee the executions. As I looked at the nooses hanging from the gallows, I had no idea who the victims would be. Finally, guards brought out the women. Their hands were tied behind their backs, and their faces were black and blue. But they held their heads high as they walked to the gallows platform, where the nooses were then placed around their necks. To prolong the agony, they were hanged one at a time. But before they died, each one of them spoke, in a clear and loud voice, two Hebrew words: *"Chazak V'Amatz"* (Be strong and courageous). These women were Ester Wajcblum, Regina Safirsztain, Ala Gertner, and Roza Robota.

They stood tall and unafraid on the gallows and died bravely. The thousands of assembled inmates were outraged and the emotion was palpable; I felt that just one outburst from someone could have transformed us into action. But we, who were already so beaten down, could only react to this indignity with a collective deep groan. I felt ashamed that we could not respond more appropriately to the heroic actions of the four women.

As soon as the hangings were complete, the Lagerkommandant was hastily escorted out of the camp and the SS units waded into the mass of prisoners, yelling and beating us in an attempt to move us all back into the barracks. The Nazis, with this action, were sending us the message that they were still in control. We of course were at their mercy, with no physical stamina or weapons with which to fight.

But there was a new feeling of urgency in the air. Our daily activities had slowed considerably. Many factories had closed down, and the machinery had been transported back to Germany. Military trucks were busy loading clothing, blankets, and other items from the barracks where these things were stored. The SS piled medical documents and registration cards in front of the barracks, then poured gasoline on them and burned the evidence. These fires continued burning for many days and nights. We heard rumours that the SS had blown up the three remaining gas chambers and crematoria, a development that I greeted with relief because I knew that as long as these engines of death were operational, I was at risk. The entire Auschwitz system was unravelling. Our workload in the operating room was down by almost 50 percent, and I had lots of spare time. But still I worried that I might have outlived my usefulness as a slave labourer, and I wondered what the Nazis would do to us as the Red Army drew near.

* * *

Christmas and New Year's 1944–45 were celebrated in Auschwitz I by prominent inmates and some SS soldiers in a barracks that was decorated with pine boughs, streamers, and posters that said "*Fröliche Weihnachten*" and "*Fröliche Neues Jahr.*" I joined the surgeons and doctors of barrack 21 at the celebration. Tables had been stocked with food, including salami, bloodwurst and liverwurst, cheese, bread, schnapps, and cigarettes. The guests at this party were Polish political prisoners, barracks elders, room elders, doctors, and Polish tradespeople, such as electricians and carpenters. The other participants included German and Austrian Kapos and under-Kapos. These men were criminals and asocials in their lives outside of Auschwitz, and they wore black and dark green triangles to distinguish them from other prisoners. The final group of guests were the SS Kommandants of the different work units. These were sergeants and lower ranks; there were no officers in this group. I estimated there were approximately one hundred people assembled in the room. The food was fast disappearing, and the mood was festive and the atmosphere convivial. Although I did not feel part of the celebration, the food was absolutely sustaining for me.

In the spirit of the holidays, the guests sang "O Tannenbaum" (everyone seemed to know the German version), and afterward, the Austrians sang a song called "*Wien, der Stadt meine Träume*" (Vienna, the city of my dreams). After the songs, the room became melancholy. I observed the reactions of the three main groups. The Polish political prisoners were hopeful because they realized the war was coming to an end and they believed they would soon be reunited with their families; the SS soldiers were aware of the advancing Red Army, and they knew their futures were very uncertain; and the men in the third group, the criminals and killers who were our Kapos, were sad because they had nothing to look forward to and would no longer be in positions of power. I was the odd man out in this gathering. I felt neither hopeful nor sad, but I was preoccupied with the fear that the Nazis would kill us all before they left the camp. Unless I was liberated, there would be no happy ending for me. The war was near its end, but freedom seemed so far away.

CHAPTER 19

Death March

Like many prisoners, I lived in hope that the Red Army would arrive in the next week or two and our nightmare would finally be over. On January 18, 1945, my hopes were dashed. Many inmates of satellite camps were brought into Auschwitz I, and the rumour went out that we were going to be evacuated. We didn't know where this was going to end, and whether the Germans were going to execute us or let us go.

Among the people brought in to barrack 21 were two brothers from my hometown who had been working in the coalmines at Buna, a satellite camp of Auschwitz I. They were in terrible shape and black from coal dust. They simply lay down on the floor of the barracks and said they could not get up again. I also saw, for the last time, the boy with the gunshot wound, whom Dr. Gordon had nursed back to health and taught to speak again. The boy, like the brothers, was not strong enough to join the departing prisoners. They stayed behind, and in fact were liberated one week later by the advancing Russian army.

That evening, SS men combed the camp and shouted for everyone to line up. We were told we were being moved to another camp—a move for which I had no time to prepare. I had only my light jacket and cap, but thankfully I still had my sturdy boots with their now-worn soles; many of the marchers had nothing but wooden clogs, which made it virtually impossible to walk.

It was an eerie night with fires burning all around and Russian airplanes dropping magnesium flares that lit up the camp. I could hear artillery in the distance. Before we exited through the gate, we were given a chunk of bread for our journey. Approximately twenty thousand of us were ordered to form ourselves into rows of five with our arms hooked together. Outside the gates, the SS guards and their attack dogs positioned themselves on each side of this enormous column. It was bitter cold and there was a lot of snow on the ground. I was on the outside left of my row. Those who fell out of the column were immediately shot in the head by the guards, who were determined not to leave any prisoners behind.

In the chaos of our rushed departure, I lost contact with all the doctors of barrack 21. I was alone and I realized that this march would be the ultimate test of my endurance. My body was in a cold sweat, my feet were soaking wet, and my light jacket and pants were also damp. The only thing that gave me a little warmth was a paper cement bag that I'd managed to retrieve as we passed a construction site. I ripped holes in the bottom and the two sides to create a vest, then slipped it over my head. We were constantly prodded to move faster because the SS did not want the column to stretch out too far, making it difficult to guard. The five of us in my row realized that we needed to march in unison, with our arms hooked together, in order to conserve our strength. We could not waste energy on anyone who would weigh us down, because it was difficult enough to carry our own bodies.

The second night was starless, but the snow made it possible to see the faint contours of the trees on my side of the column. On the other side, there was a large open area without trees. Suddenly I heard popping sounds coming from a distance, and I could see something that looked like fireflies coming toward us. They were tracer bullets, and I could hear the impact as they hit many marchers on my right side. Everyone panicked and pushed over to the left. I was overrun by the mob and thrown into a ditch, and many marchers landed on top of me. I was pinned down and unable to move, but I kept my cool and tried not to panic. The guards shouted for us to get up and keep marching, and the tone of their shouting suggested that they were scared of losing control of us. Those who were injured in the attack were shot on the spot.

We were the unfortunate victims of Red Army scouts, or perhaps partisans who had mistakenly taken us for retreating German army units. When I finally emerged from the ditch, I couldn't find the other four marchers from my row, so I tried to move as far as possible to the front of the column. It was more dangerous to be in the back with the stragglers, who were systematically picked off by the guards. I sweated profusely from the exertion of marching through deep snow, and my ears, hands, and nose were frostbitten. I had to find some way to protect my skin. As we marched on, I realized that one person in my row had succumbed and was dead. Before we let go of him, we stripped off his jacket and tore it into strips; I used my strips to cover my head and ears. I felt like a vulture, but I told myself that this person didn't need his jacket anymore. This was an act of self-preservation.

As the sun rose over the snow on the third day, the landscape was strangely beautiful. There were thousands of inmates in front of me and thousands behind me, and on both sides the SS guards cursed and shouted. Where were they taking us? What was the point? At midday, we exited a forested area and came to a village, where I could see houses with smoke rising from their chimneys. I thought about the warmth inside these houses and imagined normal people having their lunch. How wonderful a cup of tea would taste right then! All I could do was grab a handful of snow to keep myself sustained. As we entered the village, we were ordered to squeeze closer together because of the narrow streets. The guards were alert for people who might try to escape. I thought of the doctors from barrack 21. They could have slipped away easily because they were in their homeland and spoke the native tongue. I could not take this risk. Instead, I had to march on, and as I did, more people fell away from the column and the gunshots became more frequent. The byways in occupied Poland were strewn with the bodies of those who could not endure this death march.

Later in the day, as we neared a crossroads, I saw a farmer sitting on a sled pulled by two beautiful horses. The bells on their harness were ringing as they waited impatiently for the large column to pass. I remembered those cold winter mornings from my childhood, when farmers came to town and I would jump on the runners of their sleds to hitch a ride to school. Would I ever hitch a ride again? I grabbed another handful of snow and continued to put one foot in front of the other. Surely, I thought, we would stop soon. While I was determined to carry on, the dark nights were extremely difficult and my spirit was at a low ebb.

In the afternoon of the third day, we came to a large abandoned farm where the Nazis told us we would spend the night, our first rest stop since leaving Auschwitz. It had many stables and storage barns, and it was wonderful to rest at last. The straw on the floor of the barn gave my body a cushion that helped me survive another day. I buried myself in a pile of this heavenly smelling straw and went into a deep slumber. The following morning, I awoke to the guards shouting, "*Raus! Raus!* Line up!" For a moment, I considered hiding in a pile of straw, but I was concerned that I would be shot on the spot if discovered. As it turned out, my concern was well placed. As we lined up in formation, the SS guards combed the stables, shooting indiscriminately into the piles of straw. Any who were hiding there were killed.

We had already marched for three nights without any food, and now we were onto the fourth day. I was light-headed from hunger, and my body was not cooperating. I tried to keep my mind from deteriorating and focused on positive thoughts. The day was milder, and I could see that we were headed toward a sizeable town. By the afternoon, we were crammed into a soccer field. I lay down on my back, rested my feet against a fence, and looked up at a beautiful blue sky. I was almost able to imagine that I was catching my breath after a soccer game with my friends. An hour or two later, the SS ordered us to get back into formation and we were on the move again, this time to a railway station in a town named Loslau.

When we got to Loslau, we found a long line of forty to fifty open flat cars waiting. We were ordered to climb inside and were packed tightly together. Between the flatcars, there were several cabooses where the SS guards positioned themselves. They watched over us and shot anyone who tried to escape. The walls of the flatcars were metal and extremely cold. Everyone tried to get into the middle of the group for warmth. We started up, and as the locomotive built up speed, the wind it generated against our heads and bodies made the cold penetrate even deeper. I felt like I was in an icebox. I was in this flatcar for approximately four days, standing up, chilled to the bone, without food or toilet facilities. Many people died along the way.

At one point, I thought about a book I had read about the Orient Express, and I tried to imagine how wonderful it would be to experience that level of luxury right then. But this thought was not able to distract me for long. How many more days would this journey last? Where were we going? We travelled only during daylight hours because at night the smoke and the cinders of the locomotive would have been a giveaway for low-flying Allied fighter pilots, who bombed anything that moved on rails. Overnight, we stood at railway stations or sidings, and the SS units aggressively patrolled our transport so that no one could escape.

Standing in the cars was even worse than marching because we were in such cramped quarters. The tougher among us waited for the weaker ones to expire so that we could get some relief. We stripped these poor souls of their meagre clothing to protect our freezing heads and limbs. Because the SS did not permit us to dispose of the dead, the cadavers were left in the cars and we were forced to endure the indignity of standing on the bodies. In the mornings, before the train took off again, the SS guards and their officers were served breakfast from the kitchen car. I could smell food being cooked, and it was a terrible tease. They were fed while we were dying from starvation.

On the seventh night, the train came to a stop at a large station that was in total darkness. We heard the eerie sound of sirens as searchlights combed the skies for airplanes, and then there was a racket of anti-aircraft guns. We were right in the middle of a bombing raid, and shrapnel hit the metal sides of our flatcar. I thought that after all I had been through, I could not be killed by Allied bombers! When the raid was over, silence prevailed.

As the skies became lighter in the morning, wet snow came down, and I could make out the name Pilsen on the railway station. This told me that I was back in occupied Czechoslovakia. I began to feel more hopeful when I heard a commotion several cars behind us. I saw that there was a bridge extending over the railway tracks just down the line, and on that bridge were several people throwing chunks of bread into the flatcars below. The SS guards yelled out, "Do not throw bread! These are Jews!" but the people ignored them. Finally, the guards sprayed the bridge with their submachine guns and the people ran away. Although I was too far away to receive any bread, the actions of these people nurtured me nonetheless. Knowing that there were still kind and caring people in the world boosted my spirits and gave me new life.

We left the Pilsen station. It was January 25, 1945, and I had not had any food since we'd departed Auschwitz on January 18— seven days earlier. I was catching snowflakes on my tongue to hydrate myself. Half the people in our flatcar were now dead, and we'd pushed their bodies to one corner to give us extra space. But I couldn't ignore the frozen cadavers—they were a constant reminder of where I would wind up if the journey continued much longer. I was in need of exercise and nourishment, and the constant standing was torture on my body.

I was barely hanging on. Heavy snow was coming down on us, and all the dead bodies were blanketed in it, while we living zombies were wet to the bone. The train came through a station with a German name plaque. I wasn't sure if we were in Austria or Germany, but both felt like the lion's den. In the distance, I could see a railway bridge spanning a wide river, and someone said that this must be the Danube. The train came to a stop, and we were ordered out of the flatcars. I could see large chunks of ice floating down the river, and my first thought was that the guards were going to shoot us and dump us into the water. Why didn't the train proceed across the bridge? I had my answer as soon as I got closer and saw the twisted metalwork and missing railway ties. The bridge had been badly damaged by Allied bombings, and we were forced to make the hazardous crossing by foot. I had to pace myself while jumping over missing railway ties—it required a delicate strategy because others tried to grab at you, and that would hinder your balance. Many people fell through the missing spaces into the icy waters below and were gone. There was no margin for error. Those who got across were made to line up in formation by the SS guards, and we marched forward. Ahead of us, I could see a town. We were told to tighten up our lines as we came closer to it. A roadside sign told us we were in Mauthausen.

My first impression was of beautiful homes and storefronts with sparkling clean windows and delicate lace curtains. The structures were about three storeys high and had beautiful wooden ornamentation on the outside. For me, it was unbelievable to think that people were living in such comfort while we were in such misery, filth, and danger. I longed for a hot bath in one of these homes. I could die happily if I could just have a bath, I thought. While we marched through the town in the centre of the road, we passed three young women, each pulling a child in a sleigh. The children were all bundled up in knitted wear, toques, and scarves, and they had rosy cheeks and bright eyes. But they looked at us in horror. We were black from frostbite, dirty, and in rags, and a foul odour followed us like a stray dog. The children stared at us, but the three women refused to look our way. They totally rejected the sight of us, as if to say that they did not acknowledge the reality of what was happening right in front of them. I thought of the people in Pilsen throwing bread to us and noted the stark contrast.

We continued marching through Mauthausen, passing the vertical rise of a granite cliff. I saw inmates in striped garments hammering with chisels at the stone. This sent shivers of fear through me because I knew that I could not endure this kind of gruelling work. When we arrived at the top of the road, I saw the fortress-like entrance to KL Mauthausen concentration camp. This entrance had a large gate with tall guard towers on each side. It was a foreboding sight.

Inside the camp, we were directed to a barracks with showers. Mauthausen was overflowing with inmates who, like us, had been brought from other camps in occupied Poland. We stood outside in the freezing floodlit square for hours until several Kapos took charge of the crowd, ordering us to undress but to keep our shoes. We waited naked in the cold while groups of one hundred men at a time were sent through the showers. When it was finally my turn, it was a small pleasure to feel the warm water wash away the dirt and stench from my body. But it was over too quickly, and I was pushed naked back out into the freezing cold. It was clear this shower was not for our benefit, but to avoid transmitting disease to the SS guards.

The steam from the heat of the shower rose from our bodies, and I knew that we would soon have hypothermia. I felt the chill creeping deep inside me, and I began vigorously flailing my arms, hitting my upper body to keep my circulation going. I did this through the night without stopping. Many of the inmates around me dropped to the ground and froze to death. Finally, the next morning, those of us who were still alive were directed to a barracks. Inside, I saw several rows of people sitting on the floor with their legs spread apart. Each new person was directed to sit between someone else's outstretched legs, and then the next person would sit between his outstretched legs and so on. To feel bodies in front of and behind you was both frightening and demeaning. The entire floor was filled with this sea of humanity, and I estimated that there were at least a thousand people in this room.

I was furious—of all the hardships I had endured, this latest abomination was the most insulting. We were packed like sardines in a can. It's true that we weren't freezing cold anymore, but everyone was dead tired. If a prisoner fell asleep, his head would drop on the person in front of him and he could expect a jab in his ribs, jarring him awake. Urine and diarrhea seeped onto the floor under our buttocks, and the stench was unbearable. We weren't allowed to stand and we couldn't go outside to relieve ourselves. Just hours before, we had been given a shower to wash off the dirt that had accumulated on our bodies, and now I was sitting in urine and feces. I tried to disengage my mind and go to a place where I could ignore what was happening around me. I lost track of time. I lost control of my bodily functions. I believe that I sat in this way for two days, and then suddenly the Kapos shouted at us to get up and out of the barracks. We disentangled ourselves as quickly as possible and were again outside in the bitter cold, naked and smeared practically from head to toe in feces.

We had to form up in a single line to receive our garments: striped pants, a top, and a cap. I could tell from the odour on the garments that they had recently been disinfected with Zyklon B, the same chemical used to gas Jews in Auschwitz-Birkenau. We were told that we were going to another camp. I was happy to leave this hellhole and hoped I'd never see it again. It had been ten days since we left Auschwitz and I'd still had nothing to eat or drink. I realized that getting food and water would be the final factor in my survival.

We were marched out the gates of Mauthausen, across the treacherous bridge, and down to the railway station, where we were crammed back into boxcars. The locomotive started up and we were on the move again. A few hours later, the train slowed and eventually came to a stop. The guards opened the doors of the cattle cars and shouted *"Raus! Raus!"* A sign told me that I was in a railway station in a town called Melk, right beside the Danube River.

CHAPTER 20

Melk, Ebensee, and Liberation

O ur transport arrived at Melk on the afternoon of February 1 or 2, 1945. The railway lines and the highway were both parallel to the Danube River, which was full of ice, just as it had been at Mauthausen. The highway was busy with routine military and civilian traffic. Our transport consisted of approximately one thousand slave labourers. The guards took up position on either side of us and forced us to march uphill, through the town, and into a camp called Melk KL. This was an old First World War cavalry barracks on a hilltop offering a view of the rooftops of the town. Another hill, opposite the camp, had a long and very impressive building that I later learned was the largest Franciscan monastery in Europe.

After lengthy discussions between the SS guards and the Kapos, they divided us into groups and assigned us to various barracks. I was directed to a barracks that was already home to a number of Russian prisoners of war. I managed to communicate with them using a mix of Russian, Slovak, and German. They wanted to know which camp I came from and where I was born.

They also asked me if I knew how the war was progressing. The only news I could give them was that when we left Auschwitz I on January 18, I'd heard the sound of heavy artillery coming from the Eastern Front and assumed that the Red Army was not far away. These Russian prisoners were trained military men with large physiques, but they looked quite haggard. However, they knew how to protect themselves and each other, and they were a close-knit unit. I noticed that the Kapos dared not abuse them the way they abused us.

I thought to myself, Here I am in another camp, all alone again. I wondered how difficult it would be to adjust to the new conditions. What kind of work would I have to do, and would I be exposed to the elements? I told myself that if I could just survive the months of February and March, spring would arrive and the Red Army would emerge from the east to end this ordeal. But there were so many things to worry about, and I needed to be ready to face all challenges.

My mattress was full of powder and so filthy that I chose to sleep directly on the wooden bed planks instead. I had a dirty blanket to cover me. While it might sound strange to miss a place like Auschwitz I, I was consumed by memories of the upstairs ward in barrack 21, where I had a clean bunk, a clean blanket, and my busy daily routines. In the hospital, I felt I was part of a group of professionals who were helping our fellow prisoners, and I also had privileges that allowed me to survive. Melk, in contrast, was going to be a very dangerous and demeaning experience.

That evening, I received my first sustenance after ten days without any food—a piece of bread and a cup of ersatz coffee. This ration tasted very good to me, but it did not fill my stomach.

I was beginning to wonder how I'd managed to survive for this length of time.

The next morning we were woken up at 5 a.m. and given a cup of tea in our barracks. Inmates were organized into three equal eight-hour shifts. I was in the morning shift with fifteen hundred fellow prisoners. We lined up in the square and then were marched down to the railway station and put into boxcars with the doors locked. We travelled for about an hour and then disembarked. I found myself in a large fenced-in area with many sheds that stored machinery. I could see six large bomb-proof railway tunnels that were built into a mountainside, and a locomotive pushing fifteen to twenty boxcars into one of them. This place was a hive of activity. I learned that four of these tunnels were already in full production making aircraft parts; the other two tunnels were still being built.

The SS divided us into groups, and a man in a black cap and black overalls led my group to an area where the stone was being drilled for the last tunnel. I was handed a large air drill that I could hardly lift, and the man directed me to start drilling by pushing the handle. The vibrations of the drill shook my body, and the sound of it hitting the rock was deafening. We were drilling a stairway to the top of the tunnel in order to shape the contours of the ceiling. I felt that I had no strength to drill the rock above my head. As the rocks above were loosened, we were at constant risk of being crushed.

I later learned that the man in the black cap and overalls was from a civilian organization that was building this infrastructure for the Luftwaffe. The inmates worked here in three eight-hour shifts; when one shift was finished, the next was marched into the tunnel. After two days of this work, I told our foreman that

I could no longer lift the drill and asked him to place me on another job. He told me to retrieve all the broken drills that had accumulated in the tunnel and take them to the blacksmith's workshop for welding. This new job once again saved my life. It was cozy and warm inside the blacksmith's shop, and there was a red-hot fire burning in the forge. The blacksmith was a Russian prisoner of war named Misha.

It was approximately half a kilometre from the tunnel to the blacksmith's shop, and a conveyor belt carrying loose stone ran the full distance. I learned to jump on the conveyor belt, and that made my journey easier. The only trick was jumping off before the belt continued into a crusher, which would have meant my demise. Once I got to know Misha better, I asked him if he could make me a rig to carry a number of drills so I didn't have to hold them in my arms. He obliged by making a holder that allowed me to carry six drills at a time. Even though it was heavy, it made my job easier. I also figured out how to pace myself so there were always enough replacements for broken drills. That allowed me to spend more time in the warm blacksmith's shop. Misha also helped me when he gave me a pot and told me to fill it with clean snow, which he melted on the fire for the two of us to drink. This daily work routine continued until the end of March.

There was one building with showers and a laundry facility in Melk KL. Like Auschwitz, Melk also had a crematorium, but no gas chambers. I always gave the crematorium a wide berth because it reminded me of Birkenau. In the middle of the camp, there was a small hill where we walked on Sundays, when we did not work. In mid-March, when the weather got warmer, we all gathered on the hill, removed our jackets, and searched for lice. I was disgusted to discover thousands of tiny eggs embedded in the fabric of my jacket, which explained why I was constantly scratching myself. We spent many hours crushing the eggs between our thumbnails, like monkeys grooming themselves. Unfortunately, my efforts didn't make a dent in my lice infestation, which became worse as the warmer days made me sweat more. I hadn't been allowed to shower since my arrival in Melk, but when the camp administration became aware of the infestation, they took action to prevent a spread to their own personnel.

On the next Sunday morning, the Kapos ordered us to give up our jackets and pants so they could be disinfected, and in the afternoon, the entire camp was given a shower. Thousands of us gathered in front of the entrance to the shower. The door was only a few feet wide, and I knew from experience that there was going to be mayhem when it opened. The waiting prisoners would all try to get in at the same time. Anyone who fell on the ground would certainly be crushed by the mob. I asked myself if a shower was worth putting my life in danger, and then tried to determine where I should position myself so that I would be safe. But as soon as the door opened, I was sucked into a whirlpool of bodies. I fought with all my strength not to lose my footing or be trampled. Suddenly, I felt myself pushed up over the top of people's heads, and then I was passed toward the edge of the mob, where I fell to the ground, uninjured. Some people were not so lucky and were trampled to death under the feet of their fellow prisoners. I missed my opportunity to shower, but I was thankful to have made it out alive. A few days later, on March 15, I turned sixteen years old. Would I make it to seventeen?

* * *

As we neared the end of March 1945, the weather became increasingly warmer. I could hear sounds of bombing coming from the east, from the direction of Vienna, and I felt encouraged that the end of the war was coming closer. My thoughts turned to my home life back in Moldava, where we would have been celebrating the holiday of Purim, which commemorates the salvation of the Persian Jews from the murderous tyrant Haman. On Purim, it was our custom to share goodies with our friends and neighbours to celebrate our freedom from oppression. Our home would be filled with the enticing aroma of baked goods and delicious cooking. My mother would make chicken paprikash with all the trimmings. How long ago it seemed, and now it was only a memory for my mind to savour.

One morning after wake-up call, I felt very sick. I had stomach cramps, diarrhea, fever, and dizziness. How was I going to cope today? I simply wanted to curl up into a ball and pay the consequences. But my bunkmates hauled me out of bed and pushed me into a line to receive our breakfast tea, which I couldn't even drink. I barely managed to march from the camp to the train that took us to work. When I arrived on the site, I started to collect the broken drills from the night shift and take them to the blacksmith for welding. I told him that I was very sick, that I had diarrhea and couldn't keep anything in my stomach. He gave me a piece of charcoal to chew and swallow with a bit of water. He said it would take a few days to kill the germs in my stomach, and he told me to crawl under a bench in the shop and sleep it off in the meantime. I ate charcoal for three days and became very dehydrated. I gave my meagre rations to my bunkmates, because anything I put into my stomach would not stay there. I was so weak, I felt that I was at the tipping point.

On the third day of the sickness, while I was marching from the train to the camp after our shift, I got severe cramps in my stomach, and my bowels suddenly evacuated. In this moment, I released the poison from my body and instantly felt better. I knew that Misha's home remedy had saved me. Without his charcoal, I would not have survived this illness, and I was grateful for his help. However, my pants were a new problem to deal with. I had to walk back to camp, smelling putrid, and quickly wash the pants with cold water and no soap. The next day I wore wet pants to work, which was extremely uncomfortable.

The next day, when our shift ended and we were lining up to be counted, the civilian foreman came running up to the officer in charge and reported that someone had sabotaged the conveyor belt by cutting out two pieces to use as soles for their shoes. This was a very serious violation. The Kommandant announced that the person who had done this had one minute to step forward, but no one did. The Kommandant then ordered the SS guards to pick out every tenth person from the line and bring them forward. They skipped over me by only two people, and I breathed a giant sigh of relief. They marched the men a short distance away and then the Kommandant gave the order to fire. Ten men were murdered to set an example for the rest of us.

* * *

At the end of March 1945, I saw large groups of civilians from the direction of Vienna fleeing west by boat on the Danube. I also saw overloaded trains with people sitting on top and hanging off the sides. From the top of the hill in the camp, I saw military and civilian vehicles, buggies loaded with furniture, and

people on foot pulling handcarts full of goods—all of them fleeing the advancing Red Army and heading toward the Americans
in the west. Clearly Austrians were not accustomed to travelling
in this style.

If everyone was running away, what would happen to us slave
labourers? I hoped that our guards would simply go away and
leave us alone, but that is not what happened. The next morning,
we were marched down to the railway station to work as if it were
just another ordinary day. I collected drills and carried them to
the blacksmith's shop. Misha told me that there was no need to
work quickly because the Red Army would soon be here. "Go
and sleep under the bench," he said. Soon after, I was awakened
by the sound of shooting. I jumped up, and Misha and I looked
out the window to see a fighter plane circling around our yard at a
very low altitude, shooting at anything that moved. A locomotive
pulling boxcars full of aircraft parts emerged from the tunnel,
unaware of the fighter plane. The pilot banked around and fired
a stream of bullets into the locomotive, which exploded, creating
chaos everywhere. Misha shouted over the noise that it was a
Russian Yak fighter plane. It felt wonderful to have a front seat
for the pandemonium that a single airplane had caused.

When the coast was clear, I took my drills and went back
into the tunnel, where no one yet knew of the strafing by the
airplane in the yard. I had a feeling that the end was very near.
When our shift ended, the SS lined us up to be counted as usual,
but the evening shift did not arrive. We climbed into the boxcars and went back to the camp, where there was a buzz about
the pause in operations. I thought that if the SS made us take
another death march, at least I would not have to worry about
freezing weather this time.

The next day's wake-up call came earlier than usual, and this time the entire camp was assembled in the square. We stood for some time and then were ordered to line up in rows of five, after which we were divided into several groups. My group was taken in the direction of the railway. I took a last glimpse of the Franciscan monastery, thinking that I would never see it again, and then followed the other inmates in my group down to the banks of the Danube, where there were many barges tied to the shore. The SS crammed us into one carrying metal railway tracks. Once the barge was fully loaded with people, its openings were secured with metal covers and padlocked so we could not escape. I thought to myself, If this barge sinks, we're all doomed. Then I wondered if they intended to drown us by deliberately sinking the barges.

One tugboat pulled several of these barges, which were attached to each other with metal cables, and eventually I felt the movement of the waves on the Danube. We were headed upriver to the west. We were only a fraction of the prisoners from Melk—about one thousand people—and I figured that most of the inmates were being evacuated to other camps. The following day, the barges were tied up and we were ordered to get out. We found ourselves in Linz, Austria. I saw a large area full of bomb craters—possibly former factories. The SS marched us through the city of Linz, and after a full day's march, we bedded down for the night in a farmer's field near Gmunden. I dug around in the dirt of the field and managed to find a couple of small potatoes. I savoured them and then slept soundly through the starry night. We marched on, without any food or water, to the town of Wels. That evening, we again camped out in an open field. The following day, we walked through a town called Lambach. On the third day, the road climbed to a higher elevation; it was very warm and the column began to stretch out, with many men unable to keep up. The SS gave us one hour to rest. There were pine trees on one side of us, and on the other side the road dropped off into a valley. The scenery was beautiful, and under different circumstances this might have been a wonderful outing. When the rest period was over, we marched on and followed the road ever higher. At this point, we had been without food or water for four days, and I was desperately thirsty.

Along the sides of the road, we started seeing signs that said, "*Achtung Tiefflieger*" (Beware of enemy fighter planes). Suddenly, I heard an airplane approaching. The pilot began strafing us from the rear of the column, but he stopped suddenly and veered off when he realized we were not enemy troops. He then returned to the front of the column and tilted his wings at us in what I thought was a sort of apology. Fortunately, no one in our group suffered fatal injuries. I could see the star on the airplane and knew it was an American fighter. I thought to myself that if an American airplane could fly that low without being challenged, their army could not be far away.

We came to a sharp turn in the road and I saw an amazing scene in the valley below: a beautiful lake called Ebensee with blue water and houses and trees around the shoreline. I could see several Luftwaffe soldiers in blue uniforms leisurely rowing their girlfriends in boats on the still lake. This sight was a remarkable contrast to the prisoners around me, and I wondered how these people could enjoy this peaceful vignette while we were so downtrodden. There and then, I vowed to myself that if I survived, I would one day experience the pleasure of boating on a peaceful lake. A short while later, we entered the gates of Ebensee KL.

Ebensee KL was on a plateau encircled by mountains, and it was a stark contrast to the beautiful town and the lake situated in the valley below. I had a sense that this would be the last camp for me to endure, and that liberation could not be far off. Most of the inmates in my barracks were Greek Jews, and I once again had to go through the usual process of integration among already established inmates with their hierarchies and seniorities. In my new work unit, we were detailed to mix cement and pour it into forms to produce large tiles. Thankfully, we were not pressed to work hard, and it seemed to me that we were simply putting in time while the war wound down. It was the first week of April 1945. I was skeletal and the soles of my once-sturdy boots had large holes in them. Like most inmates, I was infested with lice. They burrowed under my skin to suck out my meagre drops of blood. They also carried the typhus bacteria from body to body. Most of the men in my barrack were sick with high fevers from typhus, and there was no medication or doctors to treat them. Many of them died in their bunks, their bodies unceremoniously carried outside and piled up in the latrine.

Around mid-April, the SS ceased distributing rations and the water system was shut down. I walked to the cistern where water was collected for extinguishing fires. It was large and had steep sides that angled down toward the bottom. Because the water level was very low, these side walls were about eight metres high. I saw several bodies floating in the cistern, and I suspected that these men had tried to get water and could not crawl back out because of the steep angle. I noticed others who had cups with a long string attached so they could retrieve some water in this way. I was surprised to see the Lichtman brothers, Gaby and Bandy, whom I knew from home. They told me that their father had died just a week before. I was happy to see them, but I also envied the fact that they had each other while I was alone. I knew they couldn't take care of me, though. I went back to the barracks and I didn't see them at Ebensee again.

The situation was desperate and there were cadavers all over the camp. There were mountains of naked bodies piled in the main square, the clothing removed by desperate living souls. People were starving to death, and some even chewed on their leather boots to get any kind of juices into their stomachs. I grew weaker and weaker, and finally I succumbed to fever. I slept for days, consumed by fever dreams. When I awoke, I dragged myself to the cistern to try to get a drink, but by then there were so many bodies floating in the water it was impossible.

A few days later, I woke up to the smell of cooking meat, a smell that was nauseating to me in my ravaged state. Several inmates sat around a small stove and watched as a pot boiled. I could not imagine how they had acquired meat, but when I crawled to the latrine where the cadavers were stacked, I noticed that some of the bodies were missing pieces from their buttocks. I put two and two together and realized what kind of meat was being cooked in the pot. Desperate people will do desperate things to survive. I crawled back to my bunk and hoped that I would not be their next meal.

The next morning, an inmate shuffled in with his wooden clogs and made a surprising announcement. He said the SS guards were no longer in the watchtower and there was a white flag flying at the main gate. Was it possible that our liberators had finally arrived? I was very sick and weak, but I marshalled my strength and climbed over bodies on the floor, determined to get out of the barracks. In that moment, I felt that getting outside meant life, and that if I stayed inside, where I was surrounded by death, I would surely perish. When I looked up and saw the white flag with my own eyes, I knew that my horrible ordeal was over. I felt as if a crushing weight was lifted off my body.

At that moment, the gate came crashing down and a tank with a white star barrelled through. What a sight it was! Several African American soldiers were sitting up on the turret, their eyes wide as they gazed in horror at the scene before them and smelled the odour of thousands of decomposing bodies. Our liberators belonged to a unit called the 761st Tank Battalion, which was attached to General George S. Patton's Third Army. Known as the Black Panthers, they had come through the Battle of the Bulge in France, but the devastation here was more horrific than any battlefield conditions they had witnessed. Had they arrived mere hours later, many more of us would have been dead. The date was May 6, 1945.

Ebensee after liberation.

Survivors of Ebensee.

CHAPTER 21

Ebensee, After Liberation

After observing the situation in Ebensee, the tank unit left and reported back to headquarters. The war would not end for another two days, and they left to liberate other camps, such as Gunskirchen and Mauthausen. After a short while, an American jeep full of officers arrived to assess the horrendous situation in Ebensee. There were decomposing bodies piled high in the square, sick and skeletal inmates who were naked or only partially clad, a typhus epidemic and lice infestation, thousands of starving people. I heard an officer on his radio discussing the next steps. For these men from the 40th Infantry Division, it was their first experience with a concentration camp full of walking skeletons. Their first act was to sanitize the camp and eliminate the typhus bacteria, and to accomplish this, all the barracks had to be burned to the ground.

I was content simply to watch the events as they unfolded. There were no more SS guards, no more Kapos, and no one could harm me. Many thoughts went through my head, and some memories of events with which I could barely cope. I realized that I would need help to get back on my feet before I could deal with any other issues, such as where I would go from here, and how I would get food and shelter.

While I lay on the ground, I could hear the sound of heavy trucks slowly coming up the road. The trucks rolled through the gates, bringing dozens of soldiers with them. The soldiers' reactions were amazing to see—they wanted to help us, but they didn't want to touch us. I felt ashamed that anyone had to see me in my filthy, helpless, demeaning condition. I felt exposed and vulnerable. The officers ordered the soldiers to spread out through the camp and assess which prisoners needed to be attended to immediately. Other trucks brought female nurses, hospital tents, mobile kitchens and supplies, and canvas cots. A big water tanker arrived, and the soldiers set up showers.

A female nurse wearing a mask picked me up. She cut off my filthy shirt and sprayed me with DDT to kill my lice infestation, then started to wash me under the showers. I felt so ashamed to be attended to in this condition, and I needed much more than one washing to remove the dirt. After the shower, I was laid on a canvas cot in the hospital tent. It was heavenly, even though all my bones ached from months of lying on wooden planks. Eventually, doctors made the rounds, examined each one of us, and recorded their findings. I had a superficial exam because there were so many patients to attend to and so many issues to be addressed elsewhere in the camp.

The kitchens were set up and meals prepared. I could smell the aroma of a stew, but I knew that I wouldn't be able to eat it. I couldn't walk and I feared getting caught in a stampede of starving people. The smell of the food brought anyone who could still walk to the kitchen, and I could hear the soldiers shouting,

"Hold it! Hold it! The food is not ready!" Nobody listened. The soldiers tried to rope off the kitchen area, but this didn't help much. One soldier took out his pistol and fired into the air. I knew that even bullets would not hold back the mob. The soldiers just did not understand that they were dealing with starving people who had lost all sense of normalcy. Eventually, they began to ladle the stew into bowls and distribute it to the inmates, who wolfed it down. Soon their bellies were protruding, and within minutes some men's stomachs had ruptured and many died on the spot. There was a terrible irony in the fact that so many had survived hunger only to die now that food was finally available. The kitchen unit quickly stopped cooking hard-to-digest proteins and turned to bread and scrambled powdered eggs to feed the liberated prisoners. In the hospital tent, I received water, crackers, and powdered milk.

My first night sleeping on the cot in the tent was a restful one. When I awoke, I saw large trucks carrying big bulldozers on trailers. The soldiers used these bulldozers to dig five deep trenches. At noon, US military police brought a group of local civilians to the trenches and told them to carry the dead, with one person holding the hands and another the feet. The townspeople were all dressed up in their Sunday best. Men wore suits and ties, and women wore summer dresses. They held scarves to their noses because of the stench; in many cases, flesh came away in their hands as they touched the bodies. The people looked horrified. When they dropped the naked cadavers into the trench, they looked like rag dolls. Somebody's father. Somebody's son or brother. Thousands of nameless bodies were disposed of in these mass graves.

The townspeople could not keep up with this work for more than two days, and the Americans determined that they had to find a faster way to complete this gruesome task. The bulldozers were then used to finish the job by pushing the corpses into the mass graves. The bodies were covered with lime and then earth. Rabbis and chaplains arrived to say prayers for all the dead.

Four days after our liberation, the doctors gave us a more thorough exam. I was taken to a civilian hospital with a few others to be checked for tuberculosis. The tests turned out to be negative, and I was brought back to the camp in my paper hospital gown. I had no clothes or shoes. My trusty boots, custom-made by Mr. Guttman from my hometown, had endured through one year of working and walking and had saved my life many times, but they'd finally fallen apart. Eventually, the army found a warehouse full of Hitler Youth shirts, breeches, and boots, and they distributed these clothes to us. How absurd it felt to wear such an outfit!

Before the camp was administered in any organized way by the American military, inmates who were still mobile were able to come and go as they pleased. Some went to forage in homes in the town of Ebensee, and they came back to the camp with civilian clothing and food. I felt quite deprived when I saw these men in normal clothes while I was in my Hitler Youth outfit. Five days after liberation, the American military closed the gates and we were no longer allowed to leave the camp.

All inmates had to go to the camp office and register with their name, birthdate, country of origin, and desired postwar destination. I worried about going home to Moldava all alone. At the time, I didn't know if it was still part of Hungary or had reverted to Czechoslovakia. Should I even try to go back? What would happen if I set out into a world that had rejected me a year before? I had troubling thoughts because I knew that even if I got back home, my family would not be there to take care of me. I was liberated, but I didn't feel free.

A month after liberation, an announcement came over the loudspeaker that a truck was leaving the next day for Czechoslovakia and Hungary, and those who came from those two countries were to leave on this transport. Thus, the decision was made for me. When the trucks arrived, I saw one with a sign for Czechoslovakia and Hungary, and I got on with about forty others. The truck left the camp and descended through the town of Ebensee and onward. I thought how lucky I was to have survived this hellhole. Never did I want to see this place again. I looked forward to returning to Czechoslovakia.

CHAPTER 22

From České Budějovice to Moldava

The truck took approximately eight hours to drive to České Budějovice, Czechoslovakia. It was a Sunday afternoon, and we disembarked in the centre of town. People sat at sidewalk cafes eating and drinking while a band played music nearby. When they saw us in our Hitler Youth shirts, a silence fell over them. From the way we looked, however, they soon realized that we were returnees from the camps. Several approached us and invited us to join them at their tables, and we were overjoyed to accept. They ordered food and drinks, which rapidly disappeared into our bellies. My digestive system was not able to cope, however, and soon I suffered stomach pain. My habit in the camp was to eat food whenever it was available because there was always the fear that tomorrow there would be none. But now this habit was wreaking havoc with my stomach.

Since I was the only one in our group of eight who spoke Slovak, the townspeople directed their questions to me. I explained that I was trying to get to my hometown near Košice (which had been called Kassa under Hungarian rule). They told me that the railway system was not fully operational because the retreating German army had blown up many bridges, and there were no scheduled times for departures and arrivals. I asked if they knew of a place where we could rest and spend the night. One man said that he'd heard something about a building offering accommodation to refugees, but he didn't know where it was. Another man invited a policeman to our table, and he offered to take us to a shelter. It felt so good to be able to trust a Czechoslovakian policeman after my experience with the anti-Semitic Hungarian gendarmes.

The two-storey shelter had several rooms set aside to house returning refugees. There were straw-filled mattresses and blankets on the floor, and a table and chairs across the room. On one wall, there was a large piece of paper where the returnees were able to record their names, the date they came to the shelter, the camp from which they had come, and the place where they were headed. I read through all the names, but I did not see anyone I knew. I added my name to the bottom of the list and provided my details, hoping that someone might discover I was still alive. After this day's excitement and my full, bloated belly, I was ready for rest. I lay down on the fresh straw mattress and fell fast asleep.

The next morning, our group discussed how to proceed with our travel plans. We had no breakfast to start the day and no funds to pay for anything, and my body was not functioning well. My feet were extremely swollen, but I was determined to put one in front of the other and keep going until I got to Moldava. The distance was unfathomable; Moldava was hundreds of kilometres away, near the Hungarian border.

A Good Samaritan arrived at the shelter mid-morning with a bag of bread and buns, which we shared among us. I asked her how to get to the railway station and told her that we wanted to get to Budapest. From there, I would travel on to Košice. She advised me to take any train going to the east—preferably one going to Brno and from there to Bratislava. From Bratislava, I would be able to find a way to get to Moldava.

The eight of us proceeded to the railway station and, after a long wait, boarded a train to Brno. We did not have to pay a fare, which was just as well because we had no money. But the trip turned out to be an enormous undertaking. Whenever the train could no longer proceed because of damaged bridges, we had to disembark and walk long distances to the next station. There, we would wait for another train and jostle with others to get a seat. In my weakened state, this journey was an ordeal, but we managed to find food and refugee shelters along the way, and we arrived in Bratislava after a week. There, we were directed to a shelter organized by the local Jewish community. They had facilities for washing our clothes and ourselves, and we could stay an extra day before moving on. This time, when I checked the list of returnees from the camps, I spotted the name of Chaim (Tibor) Lazarovits, my first cousin on my father's side of the family. He was about two years younger than I, and he had signed in a month earlier. It felt good to know that at least one member of my family was alive, but I had no idea how to find him.

I noticed that I was becoming increasingly bloated and heavy-looking, and it was certainly not due to the frugal portions of food that I had consumed. I couldn't button up my shirt, the legs of the corduroy breeches were too tight, and my feet were so swollen that I could no longer fit them into my boots. I knew I had to do something before leaving for the next stage of the journey. I managed to borrow some scissors and a knife to cut off the upper part of the boots and make them into slippers, and then I tied a string around the heel so they would stay in place as I walked. I cut the legs off the breeches and the sleeves off the shirt, but I still couldn't button it up. I knew that if I didn't soon stop and rest my body, I would not be able to endure much more. My spirit was willing to push on, but my body was not cooperating.

When we arrived in Budapest, I parted company with the other seven guys from my group. The railway station was a large facility with many tracks and a lot of people milling around. I was alone again and could not figure out where to go. When I asked an attendant for assistance, he directed me to a Russian troop train headed to Slovakia and then on to the Soviet Union. This was my only option because there was no civilian train traffic to Košice at that time. I boarded one of the cars and saw it was full of raucous soldiers who were drinking and carousing. They asked me who I was and what I was doing on their train. I explained that I was a survivor of the Nazi concentration camps, and that I was trying to reach my home near Košice. I worried that if the train did not stop there, I might wind up in the Soviet Union. I knew I wasn't in any shape to endure another adventure.

The Russian soldiers made a space for me on the bench and passed around a bottle of vodka with a jar of pickles. They told me to take a bite of pickle and wash it down with a swig of vodka, and that way I would never get drunk. I knew they would be insulted if I didn't drink with them, so I participated, even though it clearly wouldn't be good for my health. After taking a small bite of the pickle and a little vodka, I passed both along to the next person. The party continued for a long time. The soldiers were happy to be returning home after driving the Nazis all the way back to Berlin. It was dark outside, and eventually the drinking and talking petered off. Soon I could hear only the sound of the soldiers snoring and railway cars clicking on the tracks.

My chest ached with pain and I could only sit upright. I couldn't sleep, so I took stock of the events of the past year. I knew I would soon confront the reality of my losses, and the thought of that frightened me almost as much as anything else I had faced. I sat squeezed between the soldiers like a block of wood in a vise, and I dared not make a movement to disturb them. I finally dozed off from mental and physical exhaustion, and when I awoke, the morning sun was breaking and I knew that soon we would arrive in Košice.

The soldiers woke up, stretched, and joined the long line to the railcar's toilet. I realized that I would have to wait until I got off the train to relieve myself. Through the window, I could see houses, orchards, and buggies on the road, and as the train finally slowed down, I saw the sign for Košice. I said goodbye to the soldiers and thanked them for their hospitality, and then I got off the train and went into the station. I looked at the large clock. It was 10 a.m., the middle of July 1945.

I remembered that immediately outside the station there was a pedestrian bridge that passed over the Hornád River and led into a beautiful park with mature trees, flowerbeds, and benches. I couldn't wait to take shelter under one of those trees and simply take in the beauty of nature, with its luscious smells and sights and sounds. It was balm for my soul and I welcomed the seclusion from public view. I realized that my appearance did not suit a civilized world, but I also wanted to be alone so that I could figure out how to get to my home, which was still fifty kilometres away. I also wondered if I should go into the centre of Košice to look for the cousins I had lodged with when I was apprenticing here.

I decided to walk to the Friedmans' restaurant to see if it was open. If it wasn't, I would go to their apartment, and if I didn't find anyone there, I would go to the open-air market where farmers brought their livestock and produce to sell. Košice was a beautiful city with a large Jewish community, but I wondered how many of them had survived. With my decrepit appearance, I felt exposed and vulnerable as I walked around. The restaurant was closed up, and I was upset to find strangers occupying the Friedmans' apartment. At the market, people looked askance at me and gave me a wide berth. The farmers had all kinds of food for sale, but I had no money to buy anything. I told myself that I had experienced worse things in the past year and looks could not hurt me. I searched for anyone I knew, hoping to see someone from Moldava. Finally, I spotted a farmer who lived a few kilometres from my home, and I asked if he would give me a ride in his buggy. At first, he wasn't very responsive. But I remembered that he used to buy lumber from my grandfather on credit, and I thought that he might still owe money. I asked him to consider the ride a favour to my grandfather. He relented, but this awkward exchange gave me a taste of what I could expect when I reached home.

When the farmer had sold his last item, he told me to climb up into his empty wagon and we started down the road to my town. As we mounted a hill, I could see the brickyard where my family and I had been interned before being shipped to Auschwitz just over a year before. I could see the sheds full of dried bricks, the large chimney of the power plant, and the railway tracks that carried us away. Faced with this reminder, I felt apprehensive about returning to my former home. Then I recalled the journey I'd made with my mother, my two brothers, and my aunt in 1942, and I remembered how excited I had been to walk home from the station. The first to greet me then was my dog Farkas, and I began to fantasize about a similar homecoming as the farmer's wagon moved along the road at a leisurely pace. In fact, during my incarceration in Auschwitz and the other camps, the hope of being reunited with my beloved and loyal friend Farkas kept me going. Finally we crested a hill, and I could see my home in the near distance. The farmer had to turn off the road to get to his own house, so I climbed down off the wagon and continued on foot. During the entire journey to the town, we did not exchange a single word. When he ate some food, he didn't offer me any, and he never asked what had happened to my grandfather and the rest of my family.

I crossed the railway tracks a short distance from my home, and I could clearly see the yard in the distance. Had Farkas still been there, he would have flown through the gates to greet me. But he did not come. I stood there consumed by numbness and total silence, remembering how this was once a busy place filled with the sounds of people going about their daily tasks, chickens and ducks roaming in the yard, and Farkas and our two fox terriers providing security.

The house was still there, but there was not a living being anywhere near it. It seemed like a place with no soul. I saw my family in my mind's eye and thought of each person I had lost. It was a shattering feeling of finality, and I asked myself how I could pick myself up and go on. But then I remembered my father imploring me to tell the world what happened at Auschwitz, and it inspired me to continue. I went up the stairs to the porch and opened the door to my mother's kitchen. I saw the familiar credenza where she'd stored her dishes. And beside it, I saw a neighbour sitting at my mother's table. This woman didn't recognize me because my appearance had changed so drastically. When I told her who I was, she became angry. When I asked for water, she refused and told me to go away.

In my physically and emotionally weakened condition, I was unable to stand up to her. I had no support system, no one to help me prove my rightful claim to my family home. I left the house and walked to the town centre, hoping to find a familiar face to offer shelter and nourishment. Our former neighbour, Ily, who had lived across the street and was a good friend to my mother, did not appear to be living there anymore. I wanted badly to connect with her because I knew I could depend on her.

I was fearful as I walked toward the centre of the town. I recalled what people had shouted at us and thrown at us as we walked from the school to the railway station during our deportation. But the people I passed on the street ignored me, and familiar Jewish homes were now occupied with unfamiliar faces. These new occupants seemed quite content working in their gardens, and they appeared to view these homes as rightly theirs. Since no one stopped to offer me help, I felt there was no empathy for my sickly appearance, which increased my anxiety.

As I continued into town, I passed the building where the Bodner family had once operated a bicycle store and repair shop. There, I found one of the Bodner brothers in the living quarters behind the store. I learned that he had been a partisan, and that he'd returned to the town in February 1945. When I asked him who else had come back, he said that Gabriel and Bandy Lichtman, the brothers I'd seen in Ebensee, had returned and were living in a home in town. He also told me that Ily's husband was now the mayor and they lived in a prominent house nearby.

I went immediately to Ily's home, remembering the beautiful music that she had once played. I felt ashamed to present myself in such sorry shape, and she was shocked when she saw me. But she gave me a big hug and said my name in an endearing way that signalled closeness. It felt so wonderful to be received in this way. She looked me over from top to bottom and began to heat water for a bath. I was mortified to take off my rags and let Ily see how filthy I was. She checked my head and found lice in my short hair. She noticed my bloated body and asked me if I was ill. I told her that I had pains in my chest and could not breathe well, and that I could only sleep in a sitting position. While the water was heating for the bath, she used a chemical to wash my hair and kill the lice. Once I was in the tub, she poured water over my body to clean me and said that while I dried myself, she would get me some clothes to wear. She brought me underwear and socks, neither of which I had worn for the past fifteen months. For the first time in over a year, I felt like a human being again.

After my bath, I was ready to collapse. Ily made up a bed with lots of pillows so that I could sleep in a sitting position, and she told me that she would take me to the doctor in the morning. I had a restless night with horrible dreams, and I couldn't figure out where I was when I awoke. I could hear birds in the bushes outside and smell the aroma of coffee being brewed. Surrounded by all these comforts, I was consumed by disbelief. I had breakfast with Ily and her son, Nori, on the porch, where I was able to observe their beautiful gardens. When she asked how I felt, I told her that I was still having very bad chest pain. She said she would take me to the doctor in a few hours; in the meantime, I went to find the Lichtman brothers.

I had last seen Gaby and Bandy in Ebensee, but they had been in much better physical condition than I was and able to head home right after liberation. I was happy to see them again, but still felt envious that they had each other and I was by myself. They were now in relatively good health, and we immediately began discussing how we could start up our lives again. It was clear that there was no future for us in this town. I asked them to go with me to my house because I wanted to find out about my dogs, especially Farkas. They agreed to accompany me, and with their support, I again faced the woman who now lived in my home. I asked her if she knew what happened to our three dogs, but she told me she knew nothing.

The three of us took a walk into the orchard, which was in total disarray. The trees had not been pruned, and many of them had been damaged by large vehicles that were apparently sheltered beneath them. The whole orchard appeared to have been destroyed by retreating Nazi armoured units, and we had to be careful not to step on the bullets and mortar shells scattered across the fields. It was devastating to think of how much care my grandfather and I had once taken to nurture bountiful fruit from the trees.

Suddenly, I noticed some movement in an area of thick lilac bushes, and I walked over to see what was there. It was our fox terrier, Ali, hiding in the bushes. All his fur was gone and he was full of scabs, and when I called his name, he would not come. I couldn't bear to leave him suffering in this terrible condition, and I discussed with the Lichtmans what to do. Bandy told me he knew a hunter in town, and we went to him and asked if he could end Ali's suffering with his gun. He agreed. I returned with him to the spot where Ali was hiding, and with a single shot, the hunter put him out of his misery. As I looked at Ali's lifeless body, I knew he was the final remnant of a place that was no longer mine. I had nothing else to do here, no tangible ties to this place—only memories. I had no money to pay the hunter for his services, but I asked him nonetheless if he would help me dig a grave. He understood my situation and agreed. Together, we buried Ali as a final tribute to my past life.

CHAPTER 23

Emotional and Physical Healing

ly took me to the doctor's office to attend to my chest pain and my swollen body, both of which were making me increasingly uncomfortable. The doctor gave me a thorough examination and concluded that I had a serious case of wet pleurisy. He said it was life-threatening and had to be treated immediately. I had to get myself to the hospital in Košice, approximately fifty kilometres away. Ily went to a farmer she knew well and asked him to take me to the hospital. He agreed, but his horses had just finished a full day's work, and they needed food and rest. He said that I would have to wait until 11 p.m., at which time he would come and pick me up at Ily's home. Ily asked him to have lots of straw in the wagon so that I would be more comfortable.

While we were waiting together for the farmer's arrival, Ily asked me what had happened to my family. She had heard of terrible things. I was not prepared to speak about past events, so I told her only that everyone in the family was dead. At that time, I could not yet fully comprehend the magnitude of the destruction of Jewish culture and people in continental Europe, nor could I articulate the depth of my trauma or put my losses into words.

She described how people had fought over our possessions once we were gone. The livestock were captured and removed, but she didn't know what had happened to my dogs. She also told me that the synagogue was desecrated and the Torah scrolls were taken out of the arc and cut into pieces, or worse. The prayer books and Talmudic books were burned. Ily and I tried to reminisce about the good times. I told her how I remembered her playing the piano during summer evenings when the windows were open, and how much the music had meant to me. She spontaneously offered to play her favourite Chopin piece, Nocturne in E-flat major. I felt the music in every fibre of my body. I closed my eyes and felt as if I were floating. I was at peace, and I will forever remember Ily's kindness to me in that crucial moment. Then she brought out an envelope with two pictures that she had been able to save after our home was ransacked. I felt that I had been given the biggest treasure, but unfortunately I had nowhere to keep them. We decided that for safekeeping, she would either keep the pictures until I came out of the hospital or would take them to her mother in Košice.

At 11 p.m., the farmer arrived with his wagon and helped me get onto a thick layer of straw, facing forward, with a lot of straw behind my back. I thanked Ily profusely for all she had done, and she promised to come and visit me in the hospital. She was the only bright light I had encountered upon my return. Her kindness and caring were genuine, and I knew it was how my mother would have reacted in the same situation.

The town was very quiet, with only a few streetlights lit along the main street. The buggy had a carbide lamp rigged on each side to provide light and to signal to others that we were there. It was a beautiful, starry night and I was ready to be attended to. I knew that my body needed help. The driver and I did not converse. He may have nodded off, but the horses kept trotting at a steady pace. The sound of their hoofs seemed like a fairy tale. The journey took six or seven hours.

The sun came up from the east, and it was a beautiful morning. About an hour later, we arrived at the St. Elizabeth Hospital in Košice. The driver got down from the wagon and helped me get off. I thanked him for his time and walked into the reception area of the hospital for processing. A nun took me to a public ward, where I was assigned to a bed; she gave me a gown and took away my clothes and shoes. I got into a bed with clean sheets and a raised back that allowed me to sit up. Being in such clean surroundings felt like a luxury, and my thoughts returned to barrack 21 in Auschwitz, where there were no comforts and the outlook for recovery was so bleak.

A short time later, two doctors came into the ward to make their rounds. They examined me and confirmed that I had wet pleurisy. Then they advised me that a nurse would soon arrive to perform the procedure to remove the water. I was ready to receive whatever treatment was needed. A very kind nurse came in with a bucket and a big syringe with a large needle attached. I had never seen a syringe and needle that large in the Auschwitz operating room. She told me that the procedure would be painful, but it was the only way to gradually remove the water from my lungs and my chest cavity. She told me to raise my arms over my head, and then she positioned herself behind me, inserted the needle between my ribs, and began siphoning the water into the bucket. It was very painful, particularly when I took a breath, and the needle felt as if it were piercing my lungs.

This procedure took some time, and when she was done, the nurse marked the water level with iodine on my chest. She repeated the procedure daily for about a week, until the water was completely removed from my lungs. The doctors put me on a liquid and salt-free diet, and by the end of the second week, I looked almost skeletal. I was weak and had no muscle strength at all. I felt that my body had to be rebuilt from scratch to function normally. After the second week, I was allowed to eat solid foods and I began walking outside in the park in the warm summer air. Gradually, my body strengthened, and I felt more alive and healthier than I had in a very long time.

During my recovery, some volunteers from the local Jewish community came to visit. They took my particulars, kept me company, brought me fruit, and asked me if I had any relatives. I explained that I had seen the name of my cousin Chaim Lazarovits on a list on my way back from Ebensee, but that I didn't know his whereabouts. They said they would post my name in the small synagogue in town, and a few days later, I received a visit from a Mr. Joseph Gottlieb. He told me that his late wife's mother and my grandfather were brother and sister. He said that when I was released from the hospital, he wanted me to come and stay with them. I was relieved to know that I would have a roof over my head.

Joseph's son, Itzhak, soon came to visit me as well. Itzhak was my age, and we developed a good rapport and became fast friends. He was apprenticing to become a tool-and-die maker, and he was occupied with learning his trade. He also belonged to a survivors' group of Jewish teenagers run by the Mizrachi

Organization. With Itzhak's encouragement, I also joined this group, and to my great surprise found that my cousin Chaim was already a member. Here I got to know other teenagers as well and participated in their activities. The leaders of the group channelled our behaviour in a professional manner, understanding that we all needed help to adjust to life postwar. I struggled, in particular, with learning to trust again, and engaging and cooperating with others.

The Gottlieb family consisted of Joseph and his second wife, Malvinka; their three daughters, Ilonka, Clari, and Shari; and their son, Itzhak. There was also a cousin named Ruty and a friend named Magda residing in the home. It was a very lively and busy household. Malvinka was a wonderful cook with a heart of gold, and I managed to put on weight during the months I lived there. Feeling accepted as part of a family contributed greatly to my recovery from the pleurisy, and I began to feel like a normal teenager for the first time in more than a year.

CHAPTER 24

Marienbad

During my time with the Mizrachi Organization, I befriended a boy named Mike, who told me about a school for orphans that was soon to open in the city of Marienbad, not far from Prague. I decided on the spot that I would join him there, and I became excited about the opportunity to resume my education. We arrived in Marienbad by train in the spring of 1946 and made our way to a *pensione* called Rienzi, a multi-storey building with approximately thirty double-occupancy rooms, each with a tub, a toilet, and a bidet. When I first saw the bidet, I was encouraged by some of the other students to bend over and have a closer look, and I was subsequently met with a stream of water in the face. Apparently this was a prank played on all new arrivals, a playful initiation that all the new students endured.

Together, we were thirty or so bright boys, mainly from Slovakia, but also from Hungary and Romania. We all came from different backgrounds, and there were some initial conflicts and misunderstandings that were taken out on the furniture, which suffered a lot of damage the first year. Getting rid of pent-up anger was a necessary part of our decompression process. Rabbi Stern, an easygoing man, had come from Budapest to oversee the school. He kept us focused on our lessons mornings and afternoons, but he also gave us the space to go through this rough stage and learn to resolve our problems on our own. Eventually we all settled down, developed mutual respect, and became like a family. We knew we had a good environment to live in and didn't want to mess it up, so we became responsible and civilized.

We lived in Rienzi for three years courtesy of the town and our benefactors, and we were grateful to have a safe and secure environment. The American Jewish Joint Distribution Committee (JDC) provided all our food, and a husband-and-wife couple did the cooking and stayed with us the entire time I was there. I remember that large cans of peaches and white tuna fish in oil were especially well received because we craved protein and sweet treats. The JDC occasionally supplied large bales of used clothing from America, and I selected for myself a couple of pairs of pants with a zippered fly (a novelty for me—I was accustomed to a buttoned fly), shirts with dome fasteners, and a beautiful navy-blue fedora hat made by Borsalino that I cherished.

I was eager to advance myself and I wanted to learn a trade and be trained for a future vocation. Since I had the experience of working in an operating room—sterilizing instruments and preparing patients for surgery—I thought I would like to become a dental technician. Dentists in Europe had their own labs and employed a master technician to make the dentures, crowns, inlays, and so on. I was hired by a local dentist to be an apprentice, earning a minimal sum of money but grateful for the learning opportunity. My teacher was Herr Tutz, a master dental technician. He took me under his wing and taught me the fine details of the trade. We were together every day for almost three years. We became good friends, and he took a strong interest in me. He realized I had good hands and an aptitude for dentistry work. My future in this field looked promising.

With the stability of my apprenticeship, I was able to look upon Marienbad as a place of healing. The town was located in an idyllic mountain setting, and it had many therapeutic springs. It was named after the Austro-Hungarian empress Maria Theresa, and it was, and still is, a world-famous spa town. Wealthy people and royals from King George V to the maharajas of India all visited the spa to take the baths and drink the waters. They stayed in beautiful, elegant hotels and strolled the large baroque promenade in the middle of the town. Magnificent chestnut trees encircled the town, and each day at noon and again in the evening a full orchestra played classical music for two hours at a time. People strolled the promenade for hours, listening to the music while sipping their mineral water from cups with built-in porcelain siphons. The season there began in June and went until mid-September. Each year, I eagerly awaited the new season so I could meet new people and listen to the beautiful music. After the season ended, all the hotels closed and the staff and tourists disappeared, and I was sad to see the summer pass.

My daily routine was comfortingly predictable. I worked until noon at the dental office, had a fast lunch at Rienzi, and then rushed to the promenade for an hour and a half to listen to the orchestra play Mozart, Wagner, Beethoven, all the classics. It was a spectacle to watch people from around the world in their fine attire, and in my three years in Marienbad, I rarely missed a day of music during the open season. After lunch, I went back to work for the afternoon. I became a voracious reader and learned much about the world that I had missed out on. I read the classics and improved my vocabulary and knowledge. On some days, I went hiking in the mountains with a group of friends. We liked to challenge ourselves with daring leaps down steep paths as we descended. There was a lake where we could swim and fields where we played soccer.

In the winter there was a lot of snow and no vehicle traffic on the roads. In the first year, we discovered a huge bobsled in the shed of our residence. Wheels spun inside our heads, and we imagined how exciting it would be to take a run down the road on this beast. Obviously we could not do it in daytime; we didn't know who owned the bobsled, and we certainly couldn't get permission to use it anyway. Six of us worked out a plan to hire a local truck driver to take the sled up a serpentine road to the top of a hill. We snuck out of our rooms when all was quiet and went out to the shed, where we loaded the sled onto the truck. The driver took us up to the top of the road, where we unloaded the sled and prepared to take our first run. We asked him to follow us so we could go back up again. The heavy sled held six, and it had a steering wheel, steel runners, and brakes. With some trepidation, we all jumped on and were away! It was dark that night and the sled kept picking up speed. Our brakeman aggressively applied the brakes at every turn to slow us down. We finished the first run and completed two more, increasing the speed each time as our confidence grew. This was a huge excitement for us, but we didn't want to press our luck. We called it a night after the third run and returned to our residence before our absence was noted. We repeated this many times during the winter of 1946–47, and by the time spring came, we were accomplished bobsledders.

The following year, we renewed our bobsledding adventures. One night toward the end of winter, we went out when the roads were not as covered with snow. On the way to the top of the mountain, we noticed ice on the road—that meant the speed going downhill would be much faster. Against our better judgment, we decided to go for it. On the way down, we picked up a lot of momentum, and we weren't able to slow ourselves adequately. When we reached a sharp turn in the road, we lost control. The sled hit a retaining wall and the impact was jarring. Bodies flew all over the roadside. I felt for my limbs and quickly realized that I was not injured. Fortunately no one else was either, but the sled was completely destroyed. We pulled the broken sled down the road and stowed it in the shed, covering it with a pile of old furniture and hoping there wouldn't be any consequences.

Around this time, Rabbi Stern and some of the other students began to consider their future plans. The rabbi told us that he had a visa to go the United States and was planning to leave the coming summer. Other students had relatives overseas and were also getting ready to leave, so we knew the school would be closed by the fall of 1948. For an orphan like me, it was a very unsettling time because it felt as if everyone else was leaving and I didn't know where I would end up. Even my friend Mike had a visa and planned to join his family in Australia. I didn't want to be left behind.

Rabbi Stern contacted Rabbi Abraham Price in Toronto, Canada. He had helped many survivors immigrate to Canada, and now he managed to obtain Canadian permits for all of us needing passports and somewhere to go. His plan would have been successful if not for a coup in February 1948, during which the Communist Party took control of Czechoslovakia. President Edvard Beneš was arrested and jailed, along with his chiefs of staff, and Radio Prague was taken over. When we turned on the radio the next morning, we found out we were now in a Communist country. We were in complete shock, and we knew this would make it impossible for Czech citizens to leave. My only chance to leave would be as a foreigner. Thus, I knew I would need a new strategy. But what?

I needed false papers indicating I was not Czech, and since I spoke Hungarian, it was preferable to obtain Hungarian papers. Two months later, Rabbi Stern left for America and many students found other ways out. There were only a few of us left, and food supplies were dwindling. We became desperate and finally hatched a plan to get out. In late September 1948, we travelled to Prague and found a man who was known to prepare false documents, but unfortunately, there were hundreds of others ahead of us in the queue. The forger told us to leave our pictures and come back one month later. In the meantime, Rabbi Price sent visas to the Canadian embassy in Prague. As soon as we could get our new documentation, we'd be able to get out.

At end of September, the municipal authorities told us to vacate the Rienzi *pensione* immediately, and we found ourselves homeless again. I had lived in Marienbad for three years in a stable environment, and the beauty and atmosphere healed my soul. I said goodbye to Herr Tutz, who had taught me so many skills as a dental technician. I was confident that no matter where fate took me, I would put those skills to good use. Eight of us headed to the train station, and on the way I took one last look at the beautiful hotels and the promenade. I hoped that one day, I would be back in this magical place.

CHAPTER 25

Prague

After our arrival in Prague in October 1948, we asked around about cheaper hotels. Our funds were limited, and we rode the tram to an area of fleabag joints, a level of accommodation that would have to suffice for now. The country was a virtual police state and a new law limited people to only one night in a hotel; after that, you would be reported to authorities. To work around this restriction, we split up into twos and rotated every day to different hotels. Every morning, we met at Wenceslas Square, where we could mix in with the locals. We could never be sure when a plainclothes policeman might stop us for identification. There was a movie house in the square that played newsreels twenty-four hours a day, and we spent many a night there to avoid going back to our bug-infested rooms.

We went back to our document fixer on numerous occasions to see about the progress on our papers. He had a dingy office in the old city of Prague. The weather was turning cold, and we walked briskly with our collars up and our heads down, hoping not to be noticed. Each time we went back, we were told our papers were not yet ready. Some of the other boys were getting antsy and began looking for other ways out. We were now down to four, and I was getting very concerned about how long we could hold out.

On our fourth visit, we were met not by the forger but by several detectives who immediately asked for our identification papers. I presented my official papers, but the detectives also had my false documents and we were caught in the deception. One officer asked me which papers were genuine, and I told him I was a Slovak. He asked how my picture had appeared in the false document, and I told him I didn't know. He said I was under arrest, and it felt like a death sentence.

A van pulled up to the door, and the four of us and the fixer were shoved in and taken away. After a short while, we came to a stop and they ordered us out again. As I emerged from the van, I could see that we were inside an enclosed courtyard within a massive building with barred windows. This was a prison known as Karlovsky Vezeny. I was booked, searched, and asked for my last residence. I gave them the name of my hotel and told them I had nothing there but a small suitcase containing some clothing. The four of us were separated, and I was taken to a cell holding some scary characters. It seemed like the whole underworld of Prague was there: criminals, pedophiles, and thieves. These prisoners frisked me for cigarettes even after I told them I didn't have anything. I was in shock and feared for my life.

Hours later, a guard called my name and removed me from the cell. I was taken to the courtyard again, where a larger van was now waiting. There was a solid divider down the centre of this van, so I couldn't see or communicate with the other passengers. In prison parlance, it was termed the Black Maria. Talking was prohibited, and I didn't know where I was being taken or what had happened to my friends.

After a lengthy drive, the van came to a halt. A metal gate opened, allowing us entry, and closed behind us again with a loud bang. The sound sent shivers down my spine. The van doors opened and we were ordered out. My first impression was that we were inside a very large prison. It had high walls topped with barbed wire, guard towers, and a large centre building radiating wings in the shape of a star. I saw many cell windows. Each one had a number printed on the wall below it, and the guards used those numbers to identify prisoners who looked out the windows—a strictly prohibited activity. This prison was called the Pankratz, and it was a maximum-security facility exclusively for political prisoners. I was booked in, and my belt and shoelaces were removed, then I was taken to a room to be interrogated. I could see my documents in a file folder in front of the two detectives. They told me that I had committed a serious crime against the state, and that I would spend many years in prison unless I told them how I got the false papers and who else was involved. They said I would never see daylight again unless I came clean. I stuck to my initial statement: I didn't know why my picture was among the false documents, and I meant no harm to the government. I was handed a typewritten sheet and told to sign it. When I said I had to read it before I could sign, they kept telling me that it was only a formality. But I realized that in signing that sheet, I would be admitting to severe charges. It stated I was complicit in a subversive act against the government. I refused to sign. The interrogator was very angry and said, "I'm putting your file at the bottom of the drawer and it will take fifty years before anyone will look at it again." I knew that I was in big trouble and well over my head. I felt utter despair that, having survived the ordeal of the camps, I was now caught in this mess. I didn't know how, or even if, I was going to get myself out.

One of the detectives called for a guard, and I was taken to the fourth floor of the building. There were many cells on both sides with an empty central area between them. The cell to which I was taken had a large red circle painted on the door. I didn't see any other cells with this same symbol, and I didn't know what it meant. Was it a good sign or a bad sign? I later learned it was there because one of the occupants was under a death sentence.

The guard opened the door and ushered me inside. There was a three-tier bunk bed on each side of the room, a narrow table, a bench in the middle, a steel toilet, and a small window with metal bars. Five people sat on the bench staring at me, trying to assess what crime I had committed. When the guard left, I introduced myself and they asked why I was there. I told them I'd been framed with some false documents. I was eager to know who these people were, because they didn't look like criminals to me. It turned out that three of them were top officials with the Democratic Party and had been arrested by the Communists on the first night of the coup; one was a lawyer; and the fifth was a young man in his late twenties, a lieutenant in the Czech army. When I shook hands with him, I realized that all his fingers were disfigured and I worried that I might end up with a similar affliction. All five had been incarcerated for at least four months. I could feel they were distrustful of me, possibly because they suspected I was an informant. Placing a snitch was a common practice in the prison.

I was the youngest person in the cell and all the others were connected to the political arena. It took a few days of questioning before they were convinced that my story was true. It felt good to be accepted by them, and I felt that we could now coexist as a group. The men immediately explained to me how we would all live together in such close quarters. The toilet, I learned, was also used to wash clothes and bodies, and as a source of drinking water, so it was kept in pristine condition. The pine flooring was scrubbed every day. A schedule of duties was prepared weekly so that everyone knew their responsibilities. Four of the men were married and had children, but they had not been able to see or write to their families since the day they were jailed. The young man, whose name was Pavel, was single. He was head of security in Jachymov, a town near the German border where uranium was mined, and he had been arrested for allegedly supplying the Americans with maps of the mines and details of the refining process. He was constantly interrogated and tortured—all his fingers and toes had been crushed by the KGB—and he was the one sentenced to be hanged. He and I became very close.

Our cells were heated by hot water radiators, but these served another purpose as well: each evening when the lights went out, prisoners began tapping on the rads to send messages via Morse code. The sounds could be heard throughout the building, and yet the guards were helpless to do anything about it. Each morning, the inmates of individual floors were allowed out for a fifteen-minute walk. We were ordered to walk in a circle and not to talk. It was an eerie feeling to walk quietly in circles. When we got back, we realized that the guards had completely overturned our cells, searching for contraband. We were allowed to read books that orderlies brought around on carts; the selection was limited, but we just read and reread the same titles to keep our minds occupied. They also provided pencils and paper for us to write our thoughts.

Lieutenant Pavel and I became good buddies. I respected him because, despite his death sentence, he was very focused on the here and now. He and I made a chess set out of bread, and I taught him how to play. I also taught him about Judaism and the Hebrew alphabet. In the evenings, my cellmates often wanted me to tell them about my family and my experiences in the camps. Although they had heard of the camps, they had no idea what they were really like and they were shocked to learn the details. They realized that I had already served time under much harsher circumstances than they had in this prison, and they ceased to complain about their experiences as political prisoners.

We worked out a schedule for exercises, and every day we did a certain number of push-ups and sit-ups and walked two hundred times around the cell. Our diet was ample: porridge for breakfast with tea; soup for lunch with a piece of bread; tea, bread, and cheese for supper. I recall that my first Saturday evening meal was bread and a foul-smelling cheese called Quargel. I wondered who could possibly eat this malodorous mess, but I eventually developed a taste for it. The daily routine was liveable, but it took a greater toll on the men with families.

The orderlies, who were also political prisoners, ladled out our food and tried to keep us informed of events on the outside by passing us information when the guards weren't watching. We found out this way that three generals had been hanged in the yard. I had no communication with anyone outside the prison, and no one had communicated with me from the prison office either. I became deeply concerned that I would spend the rest of my life here and simply disappear.

One day a guard came to the door, called my name, and gave me a document stating that I had committed a crime against the government and would have to serve ten years in prison. This was "justice" without a trial. How could anyone survive ten years in this hole? My cellmates told me not to worry and assured me that the Americans would soon kick out the Communists. Sadly, I knew that was not going to happen, but I didn't want to crush their hopes. It was March 15, 1949—my twentieth birthday— and I was in a state of despair. I knew I'd need a miracle to get out of my current predicament.

Our other daily pastime was to induce hyperventilation, then hold our breath while someone else lifted us off our feet from behind. This would bring on a trancelike state and cause approximately twenty minutes of dreams and hallucinations. Afterward, we would discuss our dreams and try to decipher messages or signs of our salvation. These sessions always reminded me of the biblical story of Joseph, who was jailed in the Pharaoh's prison in Egypt. Like my bunkmates, Joseph was pretty good at deciphering the Pharaoh's dreams, and interestingly in mid-April, the best interpreter in our cell suggested that one of my dreams was a sign I would soon be released from prison. It was a delightful thought, but I didn't give it much credence. My cellmates, however, took the interpretation seriously and started writing notes to their families. They hid these in the lining of my shoes and made me promise to deliver them once I was free.

Days later, a guard opened our cell door, called my name, and told me to follow him. Everyone looked at me with surprised expressions, but I didn't know whether to say goodbye. I really wanted to give my friend Pavel a big hug, but it wasn't possible. The guard led me to the director's office, where I saw my friend Mike and a civilian I didn't know. The director announced that the civilian had guaranteed we would leave the country within twenty-four hours. Mike and I had to sign documents agreeing to these terms. If we didn't leave the country within that time and were rearrested, the director said, it would mean an automatic life sentence.

I was happy as punch to sign anything, as long as it got me out of prison. A guard returned my belongings, my belt, my shoelaces, and the few Czech coins I'd had in my pocket. We were taken to the main gate and let out. Freedom was an amazing feeling, and I felt sky-high. It was May 1, 1949. I had been in prison for six months, and I could now hear May Day celebrations and music in the distance. It was wonderful. We asked the man who'd liberated us where he was taking us, but he simply told us to take the train to Košice and left. We were stunned. We looked for a small restaurant to gather our thoughts and make our plans for the trip. I headed for the washroom to extract all the messages from my shoes. While I had a coffee, I checked the addresses and asked the waiter which one was closest to me. We had approximately four hours before the train departed. I didn't have time to deliver *all* of the letters individually, but I did take one to the wife of one of my inmate friends. I also knew that I would have to spend some time telling her about her husband after all the months they'd been apart. Mike and I decided to split up. He went directly to the station, and I planned to meet up with him in a couple of hours.

I found the address closest to me and rang the bell. A lady opened the door, and I told her that I'd just been released from the Pankratz, and that her husband, the lawyer, and I were cellmates. She was speechless at first, and then she peppered me with questions: "How is he? How is he doing? Is he well?" I assured her that he was well both physically and mentally. I tried to give her as much information as my time permitted. I handed her the letters and let her read her husband's first. Tears rolled down her face. I waited until she was done, and then I asked her if she could deliver the letters to the other wives because I had to leave town as soon as possible. She promised she would and asked if there was anything else she could do for me. I told her that I would appreciate a few sandwiches, and she obliged. I advised her to keep writing to the prison authorities, then I said goodbye and quickly left, feeling good that I had kept my promise to her husband and the others.

I got on the tram and headed for the railway station. I saw Mike at the spot where we had agreed to meet, and we bought our tickets and waited for the boarding call. It was a long journey from Prague to Košice—the train left at 5 p.m. and didn't arrive until the following morning. I was concerned about the police who frequently came through the cars and asked people for identification and the reason for their travel. I hoped we could avoid that situation. Once we'd passed through Bohemia and Moravia and entered Slovakia, I felt a sense of relief because the Slovakian police wouldn't be aware of our circumstances and we wouldn't be facing as much risk.

CHAPTER 26

Return to Košice

Once back in Košice, I went to stay with the Gottlieb family and Mike stayed with his father. We had a limited amount of time to find a way out of Czechoslovakia, and we looked at many possibilities for escaping the country. In the spring of 1949, an influx of Hungarian Jews had come across the border to flee Communism. A large number of them were sheltered by the Jewish community in Bratislava. We learned that the Slovak government would allow these Hungarian Jews to leave for the American zone in Austria because they were considered foreigners, and we figured this would be our opportunity to leave the country as well.

Mike and I packed up our suitcases and took the train to Bratislava, registering as Hungarian Jews at the community centre. The place was crowded with people and there wasn't much room. We found some boys and girls our age and joined up with them. We all spoke Hungarian, and it felt good to be a part of this group. We shared a feeling of excitement about our journey, but none of us knew exactly when we would depart.

The group we'd joined had come across the border from Hungary with small backpacks, whereas my friend and I each had quite a large suitcase full of belongings. We realized this obvious disparity could jeopardize our chances of getting to the American zone, because the authorities might realize that we were not really Hungarian refugees. We distributed most of our clothing among the other boys and reduced our belongings to the bare minimum. I packed my remaining clothes into a small discarded backpack that I found among a pile of empty suitcases from previous transports. Once that was done, I felt better integrated with the group, which included a beautiful red-headed girl named Tova, also a Hungarian survivor. She and I became good friends, and eventually she became my first girlfriend. I had spent my teenage years entirely with boys and men, and this was a new experience for me.

We were told by people in charge of the Jewish community that we must not leave the premises in case the police stopped us; if that happened, nobody would be able to help. Two days later, it was announced that the transport would leave that afternoon. Border police set up long tables in the community yard, and we lined up single file and put our backpacks on the table to be checked. One officer stamped the false registration paper that I had received when we arrived. After the police check, we climbed into the boxcars and the doors were closed. I wasn't afraid of this train—it was my ticket to freedom. When the train started to move, we all began singing and laughing. We knew that our destination was Vienna, and that we were leaving the Communist state behind. We had high hopes of finally making it to freedom.

Approximately two hours later, the train stopped and the doors were opened. We got out of the boxcars and saw a number of large American army trucks waiting for us. The drivers belonged to a Jewish organization called the Bricha, which was dedicated to taking Jewish teenagers out of European displaced persons camps and getting them to Israel, America, and elsewhere. Less than two weeks earlier, I'd been sitting in a prison in Prague, and now here I was on the road to Vienna.

We arrived at the American sector of Vienna and were taken immediately to a large building called the Rothschild Hospital, which was actually not a hospital at this time but a processing centre for refugees. It was the main transit point for all refugees from Vienna to different places in the West and to displaced person camps located in the American zones of Austria and Germany. We were registered and told to find a spot in the building, which was almost impossible given that people were practically hanging from the rafters. There was no privacy, and a huge number of people were packed in together. We were strongly encouraged to move on from the building to make room for others who would be coming from the east. Many people—including my girlfriend, Tova—headed by train to Genoa, Italy, to board ships bound for Israel. My friend Mike was heading for Australia, and I was planning to go to Canada.

My permit for Canada was still being held at the embassy in Prague. After making some inquiries, I found out that there was no Canadian consulate in Vienna; however, there was one in the American zone in Salzburg. This presented a problem, though. How could I get from Vienna through the Russian zone to Linz and a displaced persons (DP) camp called Ebelsberg, which was four kilometres outside of Linz in the American zone of Austria? The DP camp was the only option for food and shelter because I had no money and no means of getting any.

I sought advice from everyone I encountered. In the meantime, my friends and I did a lot of sightseeing in Vienna, the imperial city of the Austro-Hungarian Empire. We visited the Schönbrunn Palace and the Spanish Riding School and many other beautiful places. One day when we were out sightseeing, we passed a group of people who were speaking Czech. I stopped them and asked what they were doing in Vienna. As it turned out, they were also refugees seeking passage to the American zone, and I asked them how they were planning to get there. They told me there was an underground Czech organization that would help refugees cross the Russian zone for ten American dollars. They said they were leaving in a few days and gave me the address of the organization.

The next morning, I went looking for the address that was given to me. There was no sign of any kind on the door, and the group occupied only a small room. When I entered, I told them how I found out about the organization and said I needed to go to Linz in the American sector. At first, they said they couldn't help me. After they questioned me, I realized that they were afraid to trust me for fear I would report their activities. I told them that I had been a prisoner in the Pankratz prison in Prague and a survivor of the camps, and this appeared to assuage their concerns. The man in charge told me that they sent a group of ten people to the American zone every three days. This was the most they could accommodate because he had only one guide he could trust to lead each group. He said the next three groups were booked, so if I still wanted to go, I would have to wait nine more days. He asked for the ten American dollars, which I handed over to him. He told me that I would have to come to this office one day before departure for a briefing on how the overnight crossing would work. I felt a sense of relief because at least now I had a fixed day for the next step of my adventure, which would be critical. I hoped that the journey would be successful, and that we wouldn't encounter any problems.

* * *

As I counted down the days until my departure from Vienna, I reflected on how I would feel about leaving my good friend Mike, with whom I had shared many wonderful, restorative years in Marienbad. I felt that we had practically grown up together during those three formative postwar years. I had learned a lot from him, and he had truly motivated me in many ways. I would also be parting with Tova, who was lovely and kind and a wonderful companion. It was very difficult to say goodbye to her, even though I had known her for only a month. I was torn between going with her to Israel and joining my friends from the orphanage, who were already in Canada. Parting with Tova left a big hole, and I found myself alone to cope with my upcoming journey to the American zone.

After Mike and Tova left, I went for my briefing about the journey. There were nine young Czech men and me. We were told to arrive at the railway station at six the next morning. We needed to dress as if we were going for a hike, and to pack provisions such as bread, cheese, fruit, and water to last for about two days. The guide would be at the station dressed in lederhosen (leather shorts with suspenders) and a hunter's hat with bristles. We were not to talk to him, but simply to follow him when he boarded the train and spread out behind him throughout the car. We were told that when he got off, we should get off as well. We were to avoid looking like a group and to spread ourselves out as inconspicuously as possible. These precautions had to be followed because we would be going into the Russian sector and it was impossible to know who would be watching us there. While it was easy to enter the Russian sector, exiting it was harder. We would be asked to show our papers, and if the Russians were not satisfied, they could arrest us and ship us off to the Gulags in Siberia.

After the briefing, I went shopping for my food supplies and came back to the Rothschild Hospital to prepare for my trip. That evening, a few of us went out to a small restaurant and had some food. My remaining friends knew that I was leaving, and they were also preparing for journeys of their own. Early the next morning, I got up and left while the others were still asleep. At the railway station, I bought my ticket to Linz and spotted the other members of my group and the Austrian guide on the platform. We did not communicate but followed the instructions we'd been given. As the train pulled out of the station, I kept my fingers crossed and hoped for the best.

Four years earlier, after my liberation in May 1945, I'd returned home to Czechoslovakia from this very region. Now I found myself en route to a displaced persons camp near Linz for shelter until the next step of my ongoing quest to immigrate to Canada. What a drastic turn of events this was! How could I face the Austrian people, many of whom were perpetrators, collaborators, and bystanders during the Nazi era? It was hard for me to process this new reality.

The train came to a stop and our guide stood up and exited the railway car. When I stepped out of the car behind him, I had an uncanny feeling of familiarity, as if I had visited this place in a dream before. I looked for the name on the station and saw that this was Melk, where I had spent two months working in those underground tunnels as a slave labourer. I was consumed by feelings of dread and worried that I was caught up in some kind of a plot. I turned around and saw the Franciscan monastery on the hill.

The guide kept walking out of the station, and I followed despite my reservations. He led us toward a hilly, forested area. Once there, he stopped and we gathered around him. He told us that we were now in the Russian zone, and we would need to keep away from inhabited areas and Russian patrols. Our goal was to reach a town called Steyr, which was approximately sixty-five kilometres away in the American zone. It would not be easy, he said, but we were all young people and we could do it. We followed him in a single line and watched him for any signals in case of danger. There was no loud talking permitted. We walked until after sundown and then stopped at a shelter that had a roof but no walls. We lay down for the night after eating and having some water. It would have been an ideal place to make a fire and discuss the day's events, but that would have drawn unwanted attention to our group. I fell asleep and was out like a light.

In the morning, I felt someone prodding me to wake up. The guide told us that we would be starting out again in fifteen minutes, and we should have a bite to eat before we left. It was a beautiful sunny morning and we walked at a steady pace, doing approximately three kilometres per hour for many hours straight. Finally, we came to the end of a lightly treed area and stopped. It was 7 p.m. We gathered around our guide while we were still concealed by the bushes. Below us, about five hundred metres away, there was a meadow and some thick bushes that followed the edge of a stream. The guide told us that we would have to wait for a Russian horse-mounted border patrol to pass, stay hidden for another fifteen minutes after that, and then run like hell, jumping over the bushes and the stream. If we made it, we would be in the American zone. We did exactly what he said. Sure enough, two mounted guards arrived and we waited until they'd passed. I realized that this was the crucial moment, and that we had to reach the bushes to safety. We took off and ran like the wind, leaping over the bushes and flopping into a muddy stream on the other side. We were covered with mud from head to toe, but we couldn't take the time to rinse off in the water.

Now that I was safely in the American zone, I was eager to keep going because I still had to take a train from Steyr to Linz and then travel another four kilometres to the Ebelsberg DP camp. The rest of my group had other destinations. I went into the railway station in Steyr and saw that a train to Linz would be coming in half an hour. In the waiting room, I received many looks from the neatly dressed local citizens. I must have looked like I had just come in from doing a messy job making mud bricks.

The train got me to Linz at about 8 p.m., and I immediately started to walk toward the Ebelsberg DP camp. I was very tired and wanted to get there before dark. Walking through Linz, I was surprised to see how quickly the city had been rebuilt. When I came through on that river barge in 1945, there were bomb craters covering a very large part of the city.

CHAPTER 27

Ebelsberg DP Camp

I arrived at the gate of the Ebelsberg DP camp at approximately 9 p.m. The guard told me that I needed to report to the office of the UNRRA (the United Nations Relief and Rehabilitation Administration). I did so and I was told to go to a certain barracks, where I would be provided with a cot. The main office was closed, so I was told to come back the next morning to register. The first thing I needed to do was wash my muddy clothes and shoes and hang them up to dry. It had been a very long day, and I was exhausted and went immediately to sleep. The next morning, I was awakened by a vigorous discussion taking place among my barrack-mates. As it happened, they were all Hungarians, so we made our introductions and I asked them about the workings of the camp. Many of them had been there for years and were waiting for an opportunity to leave, but they couldn't obtain any permits from countries that were willing to accept them.

I went to the UNRRA office to register, and I was given an identity card. Then I walked around to familiarize myself with the camp and its layout. The barracks—approximately twenty in all—were originally built for an SS tank unit. Some of them housed married couples and children who had been born in the camp. The camp was full of people who were milling around and whose abilities were not being utilized. They did not seem very happy living under these circumstances. The gates were closed in the evening at a certain time, and after that you couldn't enter the camp. The food was very basic, but we had ample bread and cheese, and if you had money, you could supplement your diet with fruit and vegetables.

Next to the camp, there was a large army motor pool where many trucks and jeeps were parked. These belonged to the American military police. Nearby was a barracks used to store provisions. I noticed a big truck pulling into the warehouse loading area. It contained many loaves of bread and huge wheels of Emmenthal cheese. The driver was a boy approximately my age, and I asked him if I could help him unload the supplies. He said yes and introduced himself as Sandor. When the truck was empty, I got up into the cab with him and rode along as he returned it to the motor pool. I asked him if I could drive with him and help him with whatever he was doing, since I'd just arrived at the camp and didn't know anyone. I was impressed by his ability to drive this big truck and felt that I could keep myself busy by tagging along with him. He agreed.

Every second day, we drove to Salzburg to pick up provisions for the camp. The ride took approximately three hours each way. One day, I told Sandor that I had a permit to go to Canada but I needed to get to the Canadian embassy. On the next trip, he told me he would wait for me while I went to the embassy to open a file. It was June 1, 1949. The secretary was a young British woman, and she was very kind. I told her that my permit to Canada was in the Prague embassy, and she said she would arrange to have it transferred to Salzburg by diplomatic pouch. In the meantime, I needed to go for medical checkups and X-rays. She told me to come back in two or three weeks to find out the results of the medical exams and see if I had passed or not.

Ebelsberg Displaced Persons Camp, 1949. The driver, Sandor (left), and I (centre) were on the army truck hauling food supplies.

In addition to the big trucks, Sandor also had access to a jeep from the motor pool, and on weekends we drove to Salzburg and he showed me around the city. It was beautiful and I was impressed with the Mozarteum concert house. There was a Mozart festival taking place, and I could see people lining up to attend. I wanted to listen to the music, but I didn't have the means to do it. Instead, Sandor and I went swimming in the Enns River and he introduced me to my first bottle of Coca-Cola. It tasted terrible, but after the second bottle I was hooked.

I was struck by the beauty of the city, the shops full of merchandise, the restaurants and sidewalk cafes doing brisk business, and the well-dressed people on the streets. I wondered how these people had managed to rebuild their city and become so prosperous while my compatriots and I were still sitting in a DP camp.

At the end of June, I returned to the Canadian embassy to find out how my visa was progressing, only to be told that I'd been rejected because the X-ray showed a spot on my lungs. That was devastating news, and I think the secretary felt just as bad as I did. She told me to come back the next month and reapply. In July, I went to the embassy to apply for the second time. This meant that I again had to go through the process of medical examinations and X-rays. I was told that I could expect my results by the end of July.

In the meantime, the UNRRA posted notices indicating that the camp would be closed by the end of the year. This created a panic because many people had no alternative plans or places to go. Some of my friends from the orphanage in Marienbad had already arrived in Toronto, and I was in touch with them by mail. I wrote to them about the difficulties I was having getting a visa. They encouraged me to keep going. In the meantime, I kept myself busy with Sandor on both weekdays and weekends. I felt privileged to be seen in a jeep as we took our weekend trips. I also practised speaking English with Sandor, who spoke the language fluently. This helped me prepare myself for Canada. At the end of July, I returned to the embassy and was again refused entry into the country. I couldn't figure out why I and many other Jewish people from the camp were being refused.

The embassy was always full of people applying for visas. I noticed that many of the men who were applying were big and strong, and spoke Slavic languages. Some were Hungarians and some were even Frenchmen. They all seemed to be getting visas without any problems. These people, I learned, were staying at another camp a couple of kilometres from Ebelsberg. Somehow word got out that they were all former members of SS volunteer units that fought under the Nazis. Whenever I saw these men at the embassy, we never exchanged any words. Years after I arrived in Canada, I found out that in many cases, the perpetrators were allowed to immigrate to Canada and other countries before their victims.

In early October, I went back to the embassy, and the secretary looked very happy to see me. She told me that she had wonderful news. "I have your visa for Canada," she said, "and tomorrow morning you need to board the train from Salzburg to Bremerhaven, Germany, where you will get on the *Samaria*, a Cunard steamship liner bound for Canada."

I arrived in Canada on the SS *Samaria*.

CHAPTER 28

Canada

On board the *Samaria*, I was housed, along with the other displaced persons, in the hold of the ship. We slept in hammocks that hung from the ceiling, while the paying passengers above us stayed in cabins to which we never had access. We could observe the outside world through the portholes of the liner, and I recall seeing the White Cliffs of Dover as we left the English Channel and sailed out into the Atlantic Ocean. The weather was windy and the waves tossed the ship from side to side. Many people were seasick as the weather got worse, and the foul stench soon became unbearable. The crew was not able to keep up with sanitation issues, and the passengers in the hold became unruly and delirious, shouting that they wanted to get off the ship. Many had to be forcibly restrained. I began to feel nauseated, but a sailor advised me to keep eating because seasickness was worse on an empty stomach. I took his advice and went to the mess hall to eat. There were very few of us at the table.

The storm lasted for approximately eight days and then finally subsided. Afterward, we were stuck in a thick fog, and the ship's horn blared frequently to warn other vessels of our presence. Without radar, the ship had to coast along at a very slow speed to avoid collisions. Eventually, it came to a complete halt and I could see through the portholes that we were in the estuary of what I later learned was the St. Lawrence River. I could see the church spires and the citadel of Quebec City. A boat approached and a pilot came on board to bring the *Samaria* into dock. I had arrived in Canada at last.

The paying passengers were the first to disembark the ship, and then it was our turn. All the displaced persons were escorted to a terminal, and I was handed a tag with the name "Toronto" and told to wear it around my neck. There were many large signs with the names of different Canadian cities, and our destinations were determined by the organization that had sponsored our visas. Our UNRA papers were stamped with a landing certificate—it was October 25, 1949. At another table in the terminal, I received a wrapped sandwich and a cup of coffee, and I set off with this in hand to board the train to Toronto, which was ready and waiting. I was hungry and ate the sandwich immediately, not realizing how long the journey would take. The ride lasted overnight and into the next afternoon, with the train stopping at every station along the way. I had no money to purchase food from the porter and I was hungry all the way.

As I rode in the train, I wondered what lay ahead for me in Canada. I knew it would be up to me to put together a life in this country, a sobering thought that made me quite anxious. As the train continued through the night, I saw lights from dwellings and I imagined people living safe and comfortably inside. This was my dream: to live in a secure environment with a future that was up to me. From the Jack London books I had read as a child, I imagined Canada as a vast land with open skies, a relatively small population, and indigenous people in traditional dress. I wanted to live in the midst of nature, not in a huge American city like New York.

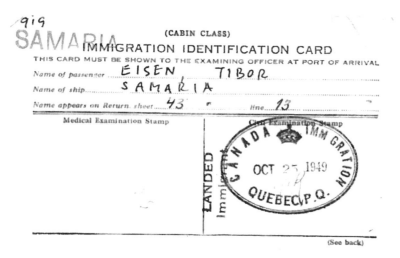

My immigration identification card, which I received when I became a landed immigrant, October 25, 1949.

When I arrived at Union Station in Toronto, I was met by a friend, Alex Weiss, who had landed a few months earlier. I had written to Alex from the DP camp about my impending arrival on the *Samaria*. It was so good to see him. We got into a taxicab and drove to the home of Mr. and Mrs. Cass, an elderly couple who opened their home to newly arrived DPs. Two of my acquaintances from Marienbad were already housed there.

Mrs. Cass showed me around the dwelling and took the time to explain the workings of the pull-chain toilet and the wall telephone. While Marienbad had modern facilities, this lodging was somewhat wanting. But Mrs. Cass had a heart of gold and she sincerely wanted to help us. From this house, I had a firm base on which to make my adjustment to a new world. I was a ward of the Jewish Family and Child Service, which provided me with a tailor-made suit and a winter coat, paid for my lodging, and even supplied a few dollars of pocket money until I found employment. This service gave me a leg up and I was grateful for it.

From the safety of Canada, I could see that postwar Europe was a tangled web of competing political systems. Countries were rebuilding, and governments were trying to re-establish a sense of normalcy on the shifting sands between totalitarianism and democracy. I had experienced the gamut of political systems, from fascism in Hungary and Nazism in the camps to a short period of democracy in postwar Czechoslovakia and a Communist takeover in 1948. During my final months in Czechoslovakia, I yearned for a home where I could have security and freedom, space to heal from the horror of the camps, and the ability to live like a normal human being. But I couldn't visualize what my dream of freedom in a new world might look like. I had only a basic knowledge of English and little formal education. For me, Canada was simply a shining bright light, a place where I could finally succeed in my quest for physical and emotional security.

In Marienbad, I'd had three years of training to be a dental technician, and I thought I wouldn't have a problem finding employment in this field. Jewish Vocational Services directed me to three dental laboratories. But none of them would hire me, even though I offered to work unpaid for a few weeks to show them my capabilities. This rejection shook me—I was trained and confident in the field, but no longer employable. I had to look for other work. Jewish Vocational Services sent me to a little shop that was willing to hire refugees. Art Bookbinding and Novelty Company manufactured wedding albums and other items, and I was hired at a starting wage of twenty-five cents an hour. A bottle of Coke was five cents, a streetcar ticket about the same, but I was happy to have a job and to be able to earn money.

The forewoman of the company, Rose Cosman, was very accommodating to new immigrants. She called me Max instead of Tibor, which I accepted because it fit better in the Canadian context and also corresponded closely to my Hebrew name, Mordecai. Rose became my mother-in-law when I married her daughter, Ivy, in 1952. She and her husband, Samuel, had first introduced us, and we have been happily married for over sixty years and have two sons, two grandchildren, and three great-grandchildren.

I am indebted to my in-laws for making my adjustment to Canada much easier. Indeed, my new extended family welcomed me so openly that I was able to integrate into the new environment and quickly adopt Canadian values of family, hard work, free expression, and leisure.

After a few years at Art Bookbinding and also trying my hand at a wholesale clothing business, I was able to start a successful manufacturing company related to bookbinding, while Ivy worked at home caring for our two sons.

At fifteen years of age, I entered Auschwitz and lost everyone I loved in a matter of months. Today, at eighty-six years of age, my heart is full again. Although I'm retired from business, I seem to work harder than ever as a Holocaust educator in schools and other institutions throughout the country. I also accompany groups to Poland for the March of the Living and on Friends of Simon Wiesenthal Center missions in order to enlighten people about the realities of the Holocaust and keep historical memory alive. It is in this way that I have fulfilled my final promise to my father: telling the story of our collective suffering so it will never be forgotten.

My wife, Ivy, and my two sons, Edmund (left) and Larry.

Epilogue

My new life in Canada was difficult in many ways. I had to learn a new language, new customs, new values. I was very fortunate to connect with people who were helpful in this journey. Soon after my arrival, I met my wife-to-be and her family, and they helped me to settle and participate more fully in my new world. I endured many challenges in those early years—juggling night school and work, dealing with the rejection of my trade skills, and labouring at menial jobs to earn money for my needs. But I always had my goal before me, which was to succeed in my quest for security.

It was not until I retired in 1988 that I had time to reflect on my past as a Holocaust survivor. Without the daily demands of work, I was able to spend time as a speaker–educator and make frequent presentations to students and adults. Going back to Holocaust sites in Europe with groups is also part of my journey. By sharing my experiences with organizations such as the local police, the provincial police, and the Canadian Forces College, I have been able to impart my knowledge of the years from 1933 to 1945 in Europe.

Johnnie Stevens of the 761st Black Panther Tank Battalion and I in New Jersey, 1999.

Now, years later, when I recount my story to young people, I often tell them how on that fateful night of Passover in April 1944, our family gathered around the Seder table in relative peace and freedom to sing songs of redemption from slavery in Egypt. Ironically, within a few hours we were reduced to a state of abject defenselessness and robbed of every single human right.

On a brighter note, in addition to keeping up a rigorous speaking schedule, I find time to relax at my cottage, where I have a CL-16 sailboat. In some way, it may have been inspired by the beautiful lake I saw during the three-day march from Linz to Ebensee concentration camp in 1945. The sight of that German airman rowing a boat with his young lady was so powerful, I told myself that if I survived, I would one day have a boat of my own.

After years of speaking as a survivor, I viewed writing my memoir as the next logical step. I was very relieved to complete a draft of the manuscript just before I left for another trip to Poland for the 2015 March of the Living. Immediately after describing my survival in Auschwitz to a group of adults, I travelled to Lüneburg, Germany, on April 21, 2015, to act as a witness in the trial of Oskar Groening, who served as an SS guard at Auschwitz II–Birkenau. Groening was accused of being present at the arrival platform in Birkenau, and of knowingly assisting in the deliberate murder of at least three hundred thousand Jews from Hungary between May 16, 1944, and July 11, 1944. Before I left the group in Auschwitz, they asked me how I would be able to face this perpetrator seventy-one years after my arrival in Birkenau. This question prompted much introspection.

Prior to the trial, I tried to visualize the defendant back in 1944, with his SS regalia and the skull-and-crossbones emblem on his hat. I knew that he would look older now, perhaps like an ordinary senior citizen. I wondered how I would feel when I first got a glimpse of him. I felt nervous and was aware of the irony of my situation—I was coming from an educational visit to Auschwitz-Birkenau to a German court with German judges guarded by German police. I felt like the ghosts of the past were with me again.

Once in Germany, I was met by lawyers and other witnesses who went over the court proceedings, and I felt more at ease. The following morning, a bus picked us up and drove us to the courthouse, where a crowd had gathered. There was a large compliment of police and press from all over Europe. To enter the courtroom, everyone had to be searched by the police, and our wallets, purses, bottles of water, and any other items were put into containers and placed into lockers. We had to show our passports, and our names were checked off a list of people permitted to enter the courtroom. There were journalists inside, along with a hundred or so members of the public. They were directed to sit in the centre of the room. Five judges sat on an elevated platform, and the four lawyers for the co-plaintiffs sat below and to the right. We, the witnesses, were seated behind our lawyers. And to the left of the judges sat the defendant, Oskar Groening, with his two lawyers. Everyone had earphones with simultaneous translation in German, English, and Hungarian.

Aided by his two lawyers, the defendant entered through a side door using a walker. I was completely fixated on him. He wore a beige pullover and an open white shirt with dark trousers. His face was sallow, his posture bent; he was both sickly looking and entirely ordinary. Once the judges entered, the chief judge, Franz Kompisch, ordered a moment of silence and then allowed us all to sit down. One of the other judges laid out the case and explained the procedural ground rules.

In 1944, when I arrived with the Hungarian transports, I could never have imagined facing off in a courtroom with a trained SS guard. Groening was charged as an accessory to the genocide at Auschwitz. In his defence, he claimed that while he was morally guilty, he was not guilty of any actual crimes. When he was asked if he was in the Hitler Youth, he answered in the affirmative. When he was asked why he later joined the SS, he said that the Führer had called the Jews a threat to Germany and he felt obliged to help the fatherland. He also mentioned that wearing the SS uniform gave him prestige and stature. He explained that after his SS training, he was assigned to camp duty in Auschwitz-Birkenau. He was known as the Bookkeeper and he was in charge of gathering valuables such as currency, jewellery, and gold crowns pulled from the mouths of gassed Hungarian

Jews. He accumulated any valuables that were collected from victims and carried it all in a metal suitcase to a bank in Berlin, twice or sometimes three times per week. When he was asked if he ever received a delivery receipt for these valuables, he said he did not. When he was asked if he ever removed any monies for his own personal use, he answered no. The prosecutors asked if he recalled giving an interview to the BBC some years earlier, during which he stated that he did in fact remove some funds to buy a pistol on the black market. When reminded of this, he replied, "Ah! I had forgotten that."

A cattle car at Auschwitz II–Birkenau.

Asked to describe his typical day on the job in 1944, he said, "That was a very busy time, when Hungarian Jews were arriving nonstop around the clock." One time, he served a twenty-four-hour shift on the ramp. Three transports were waiting to be processed, and everything had to be done speedily and in an orderly fashion. After the first transport disembarked and people were selected out, most of them were sent to the gas chambers because there was no need for slave labour at the time. He described how the Kapos and other inmates removed the luggage from the cattle cars and piled it on the platform to be loaded onto trucks and taken to the barracks known as Kanada. The cattle cars were cleaned of all debris and excrement, and left to bring more people from Hungary. Groening stated that he was on the platform to make sure nothing was stolen by the Kapos, whom he called "crooks." In a shocking piece of testimony, he volunteered that he and his comrade heard crying from one of the piles of belongings. When they walked over, his comrade uncovered a baby under a blanket. He grabbed it by the ankles and smashed its head against the metal siding of the loading truck. The "crying stopped." After this incident, Groening immediately asked for a transfer but was refused. Hearing him speak about this crime infuriated me because he described it so dispassionately. When the prosecutor asked him if a Jewish person had a chance of leaving Auschwitz-Birkenau alive, he answered in a loud, assertive tone, "Absolutely not."

On the third day of the trial, April 23, 2015, I was asked to testify about my incarceration in Auschwitz I and other camps. I told the court how my entire family was lost during the war years—my maternal family in 1942 in Majdanek, and my paternal family in Birkenau in 1944. I concluded by turning to Oskar Groening and saying: "You—who wore the uniform of the SS with the skull and crossbones on your cap, and who swore a blood oath to Hitler—you thought you were ten feet tall and could simply grind us away. Now, at ninety-three years of age, can you not do the right thing and say what needs to be said, the simple truth—that you were a part of the crimes committed?"

I felt drained after my testimony, but I was satisfied that it was part of the official record. Even after seventy-one years, a perpetrator can be judged for his or her involvement in crimes of this magnitude. The press and TV crews from Europe were all present to record the court proceedings and disseminate them for all to see. Groening wholeheartedly believed in the propaganda of the Nazi supremacist ideology, and although he was convicted and sentenced to four years in prison, he maintains that he was simply following orders and is not guilty of any crime. As Chief Justice Franz Kompisch stated, any SS man or officer who served as part of the operations in Auschwitz should be considered an accomplice to murder. After listening to Oskar Groening and observing his demeanour at the trial, I have a great deal of concern for humanity should a supremacist ideology take hold again. It will be a threat to our way of life and our freedom.

* * *

On May 8, 2015, the world commemorated the seventieth anniversary of VE day (Victory in Europe day), the Allied triumph over Nazism and fascism. I thought that the world would have heeded the lessons of the past, and that the remains of the death camps and the mass graves would be a constant reminder. However, with anti-Semitism on the rise—and so blatantly expressed in contemporary Europe—many Jews are again feeling threatened.

241

In my presentations, I speak about the lessons that each individual must internalize, and the need for vigilance to prevent hate from disrupting, distorting, and endangering our societies. We must all be alert to the dangers of hatred, speak out against discrimination, and defend the fairness and openness of a free and democratic society with rules of law to sustain it.

Looking at the Book of Names—hundreds of thousands of names—at Auschwitz I. I found my family's names among those many lost.

Each time I visit one of the many memorials to the Holocaust, I come away with the feeling that for many it is very difficult to grasp the enormity of the tragedy. One person who understood—and took personal responsibility for—this horror was Pope John XXIII. A few weeks before his death, he penned the following deeply moving penitential prayer:

We are conscious today that many, many centuries of blindness have cloaked our eyes so that we can no longer see the beauty of Thy chosen people, nor recognize in their faces the features of our privileged brethren.

We realize that the mark of Cain stands upon our foreheads. Across the centuries our brother Abel has lain in blood which we drew, or shed tears which we caused by forgetting Thy love.

Forgive us for the curse we have falsely attached to their name as Jew.

Forgive us for crucifying Thee a second time in their flesh. For, O Lord, we know not what we did.

Afterword

Tibor "Max" Eisen and his family were deported to Auschwitz-Birkenau in the spring of 1944, during the Holocaust's final phase, which targeted approximately eight hundred thousand Jews living within the wartime borders of Hungary. They were the last major Jewish community still alive in occupied Europe.* Although Hungary was allied with Nazi Germany and had introduced its own anti-Semitic laws in 1938,** the country's leaders had resisted Nazi injunctions to

---

* See Debórah Dwork and Robert Jan van Pelt, *Auschwitz: 1270 to the Present* (New York: W.W. Norton & Company, 1996), 337. Randolph L. Braham, "Foreword" in *The Holocaust in Hungary: Evolution of a Genocide,* Zoltán Vági, László Csősz, and Gábor Kádár (Lanham, MD: AltaMira Press, 2013), xvii.

** Lucy S. Dawidowicz, *The War Against the Jews, 1933–1945* (New York: Bantam Books, 1975), 381. For more on Canadian media coverage of Hungarian anti-Semitic laws, see Amanda Grzyb, "From Kristallnacht to the MS *St. Louis* Tragedy: Canadian Press Coverage of Nazi Persecution of the Jews and the Jewish Refugee Crisis, September 1938 to August 1939," in *Nazi Germany: Canadian Responses,* ed. L. Ruth Klein (Montreal and Kingston: McGill-Queen's University Press, 2012), 86–90.

deport their Jewish population to the extermination camps in Poland. In March 1942, 75 to 80 percent of the eventual victims of the Holocaust were still alive, but "a mere eleven months later, in mid-February 1943, the percentages were exactly the reverse."[*] Among the victims of this "short, intense wave of mass murder"[**] were three million Polish Jews, many of whom perished in the three Operation Reinhard extermination camps (Treblinka, Sobibór, and Bełżec) between October 1941 and November 1943.[***] The Nazis and their collaborators also deported Jews from France, Holland, Belgium, Norway, the German Reich, Luxembourg, Romania, Bulgaria, Macedonia, Slovakia, Croatia, Italy, Greece, and Serbia. Prior to their arrival at one of the six extermination camps, many European Jews endured horrific conditions in ghettos, labour camps, and transit camps, where death by starvation and disease was an everyday occurrence. On the Eastern Front, the Einsatzgruppen (Nazi mobile killing units) massacred more than one million Jews, primarily through mass shooting operations in the Nazi-occupied cities and villages of Poland, Estonia, Latvia, Lithuania, Belarus, Ukraine, and other Soviet territories.

Jews had lived in Hungary for over nineteen hundred years, with some evidence of a Jewish presence dating back to the Roman Empire. Like all other European countries, Hungary had

---

[*] Christopher R. Browning, *Ordinary Men: Reserve Police Battalion 101 and the Final Solution in Poland* (New York: HarperCollins, 1992).

[**] Ibid.

[***] Martin Gilbert, *The Routledge Atlas of the Holocaust, 3rd Edition* (London: Routledge, 2002), 90.

a long history of anti-Semitism, including instances of exile and violent pogroms, accusations of "blood libel," and orders to wear identifying badges.* There were also periods of relative tolerance: the Hungarian parliament emancipated Jews as individuals in 1867 and officially recognized the religion in 1895, granting Jews full civil rights.** At the same time, however, "a new form of political anti-Semitism emerged, integrating anticapitalist frustrations, xenophobic hatred, and religious anti-Judaism rooted in ancient superstitions."*** In May 1938, the Hungarian government began to enact anti-Semitic laws (similar to Nazi Germany's 1935 Nuremberg Laws) that severely restricted Jewish participation in Hungarian public life. Max's family fell under the jurisdiction of these laws in the spring of 1939, after the Munich Agreement (dated September 29, 1938) initiated the partition of Czechoslovakia, beginning with the Nazi annexation of the Sudetenland. Max's village of Moldava nad Bodvou in southern Czechoslovakia was annexed to Hungary, which, as Max laments, separated him from his maternal relatives, whose farm remained in Slovak territory. Although anti-Semitism was prominent in both Slovakia and Hungary, living on the Hungarian side of these new borders likely contributed to Max's survival. With the signing of the Tripartite Pact (between Germany, Italy, and Japan) in November 1940, Slovakia joined the Axis and began to par-

---

* See "Introduction: The Historical Framework," in *The Holocaust in Hungary: An Anthology of Jewish Response*, trans. and ed. Andrew Handler (Tuscaloosa: University of Alabama Press, 1982), 1–4.

** Ibid., 4.

*** Vági, Csősz, and Kádár, *The Holocaust in Hungary*, xxxv.

ticipate in the Final Solution. As early as March 1942, Slovak gendarmes, soldiers, and members of the Hlinka Guard delivered Jews to the Nazis with much enthusiasm. Max's maternal family members were among those sent to Majdanek, which functioned as a concentration camp, a death camp, and a sorting centre for the belongings confiscated from victims at Treblinka, Sobibór, and Bełżec. All of them perished there.

In the two years preceding the Hungarian deportations to Auschwitz, Prime Minister Miklós Kállay and Regent Miklós Horthy had successfully resisted Hitler's Final Solution and eased off on the anti-Semitic laws, which were no longer strictly enforced.* They also prosecuted a number of Hungarian military officers for the massacres of Jews and Serbs in the Novi Sad raid of January 1942.** By early 1944, the Allies were making significant military advances against the Axis, and Allied victory appeared inevitable. Knowing that the end of the war was imminent, Kállay and Horthy began a series of "secret" armistice negotiations with the Allies, a development of which Nazi officials were well aware. In response, the Nazis occupied Hungary on March 19, 1944, and made immediate plans to deport the Hungarian Jews to the extermination camps in occupied Poland. They forced Horthy to enact a regime change, and on March 22, Döme Sztójay was appointed prime minister with the Nazis' approval.

With Sztójay in command, the mass murder of the Hungarian Jews advanced very swiftly. From March to August, the government "introduced over one hundred anti-Jewish decrees

---

* Gilbert, *The Routledge Atlas of the Holocaust,* 184.

** Braham, "Foreword," xvii.

depriving Jews of the rights, assets and freedoms,"* all under the watchful eye of SS-Obersturmbannführer Adolf Eichmann, who had come to Hungary to oversee the deportations. By March 31, all Jews were forced to wear a yellow Star of David on their clothes. This was followed by preparations for the physical isolation of the Jews in ghettos and collection camps. Like many rural Hungarian Jews, Max and his family were not ghettoized but were transferred directly to a collection camp—the brickyard— where they stayed for only three weeks. The brickyard was one of many "camp-like accommodations outside residential areas: in factories, industrial or agricultural buildings, or other areas (mines, forests)."**

Meanwhile, in Auschwitz-Birkenau, the SS also began to plan for the influx of Hungarian Jews, which would mark the extermination camp's most lethal period. Filip Müller, a member of the Auschwitz Sonderkommando (Jewish prisoners who were forced to work in the gas chambers and crematoria), described hearing the disturbing news that trains would soon begin to arrive from Hungary: "Towards the end of April 1944 there were increasing rumours of the imminent extermination of the Jews of Hungary. To us, the prisoners of the Sonderkommando, this terrible news came as a devastating blow. Were we once more to stand by and watch while more hundreds upon thousands were done away with?"*** SS-Hauptscharführer Otto Moll, who

---

* Vági, Csősz, and Kádár, *The Holocaust in Hungary*, 73.

** Ibid., 83.

*** Filip Müller, *Eyewitness Auschwitz: Three Years in the Gas Chambers* (New York: Stein and Day, 1979), 124.

managed the Auschwitz II–Birkenau gas chambers and crematoria, forced inmates to dig two additional pits behind Crematorium 5 in preparation for a greater-than-usual volume of corpses.* The Nazis also extended the train lines inside the camp and built a new unloading ramp to accommodate the large numbers of Hungarian Jews they expected.**

When Max stepped onto that unloading ramp at the age of fifteen, he was on the cusp of the minimum age for slave labour—a possibility for survival not afforded to his younger brothers and baby sister. As he describes the final separation of his family, the reader yearns for some parting exchange between Max and his mother, but the chaos of arrival engulfed them both, and Max—and the reader—was denied this moment. As he was ushered toward the Sauna to be processed into the camp, he unknowingly had a glimpse of his family's fate when he thought he saw people jumping into the crematory pyres that Otto Moll had prepared weeks earlier. Other Hungarian survivors, including Alexander Ehrmann, describe a similar state of confusion: "Beyond the barbed-wire fences there were piles of rubble and branches, pine tree branches and rubble burning, slowly burning. We were walking by, and the sentries kept on screaming, '*Lauf! Lauf!*' and I heard a baby crying. The baby was crying somewhere in the distance and I couldn't stop and look. We moved, and it smelled, a horrible stench. I knew that things in the fire were moving, there were babies in the fire."***

---

* Dwórk and van Pelt, *Auschwitz*, 338.

** Ibid.

*** Ibid., 341–42.

Auschwitz was not a single place but a network of camps in the Nazi-occupied Polish town of Oświęcim. It included the extermination camp at Auschwitz II–Birkenau; the labour camps at Auschwitz I and Auschwitz III–Monowitz; and other satellite worksites and factories. Today, Auschwitz is the most iconic symbol of the Holocaust, in part because it had the largest number of victims (1.1 million, mostly Jews), and in part because a relatively large number of survivors (tens of thousands) were left to transmit the stories of suffering there. At Treblinka, by comparison, nearly as many Jews and Romani were murdered (as many as 900,000), and less than eighty survived. Bełżec and Chełmno had only two known survivors each. Countless oral and written testimonies have inscribed Auschwitz into our collective consciousness, including Elie Wiesel's *Night*, Primo Levi's *Survival in Auschwitz*, and Art Spiegelman's *Maus*, as well as numerous films.

While Max joins a chorus of Auschwitz survivors and some of his references may be familiar to the reader (the selection process at Birkenau, standing for hours at roll call, the prisoner orchestra in Auschwitz I, and the daily hunger, humiliation, and exhaustion), his account of daily life in the hospital of barrack 21 offers a wholly unique perspective on the procedures and processes of the camp. His description of the medical operations (both official and illicit) performed in the surgery ward gives us a glimpse into the complex role that prisoner doctors played in healing and resistance.

Many readers will be familiar with Josef Mengele, the infamous Nazi doctor who performed the selections on the unloading ramp and engaged in medical experimentation on prisoners, sometimes for pseudo-scientific "research," and sometimes for clinical trials for chemical and pharmaceutical products.* Indeed, the death in Auschwitz of each member of Max's immediate family was tied in some way to a Nazi doctor: his mother, siblings, and grandparents were selected for gassing by a Nazi doctor on the unloading ramp in Birkenau, and his father and uncle were later selected for medical experimentation by Nazi doctors at Auschwitz I. Fewer readers will know about the prisoner doctors who worked in official and unofficial capacities through the camp. In *The Nazi Doctors*, psychiatrist Robert Jay Lifton details the difficult position of these men and women: "For prisoner doctors to remain healers was profoundly heroic and equally paradoxical: heroic in their combating the overwhelming Auschwitz current of murder; paradoxical in having to depend upon those who had abandoned healing for killing—the Nazi doctors."**

Through Max's account, we come to know one of these heroic prisoner doctors: Dr. Tadeusz Orzeszko, the Polish political prisoner who mysteriously saved Max from certain death in the gas chamber and assisted the resistance movement at great personal risk. Dr. Orzeszko was born in Tashkent (now in Uzbekistan but then part of Turkestan) in 1907. He attended medical school in Warsaw, worked as a general practitioner and OB-GYN assistant in Radom (also in Poland), and began to study surgery in 1937. When Germany invaded Poland on September 1, 1939, triggering the Second World War, Orzeszko aided members of the Polish underground and eventually joined the Union of

---

* See Robert Jay Lifton, *The Nazi Doctors: Medical Killing and the Psychology of Genocide* (New York: Basic Books, 1986); and *Przeglad Lekarski: Auschwitz* (XVIII, Series II), (Warsaw: State Medical Publishers, 1962).

** Lifton, *The Nazi Doctors*, 214.

Armed Struggle in 1940.[*] In addition to providing illicit medical assistance to partisans, he engaged in intelligence gathering and distributed resistance media. The Gestapo arrested Orzeszko in April 1943, tortured him for months, and eventually deported him to Auschwitz. Like Max, he first entered barrack 21 as a patient and was eventually employed there.[**]

Max was separated from Orzeszko during the death march and knew nothing of his fate, but the doctor also made it to Mauthausen alive. Although Max was quickly transferred to Melk and Ebensee, Orzeszko remained at Mauthausen, where he also worked as a camp physician, until his liberation. Max did not see the doctor again before his death, but he did meet his family members in Warsaw in March 2010 at a reception organized by the Toronto-based Friends of Simon Wiesenthal Center. He has since maintained a close friendship with Orzeszko's son, Jan, and he recently learned that Dr. Orzeszko's granddaughter, Julia, named her baby son Max in his honour.

In addition to the details of the surgery ward in barrack 21, Max's memoir also provides a unique perspective on "liberation" as both an acute moment of freedom and a long, arduous process of recovery marred by illness, overwhelming grief, and years of displacement and uncertainty. It is striking that Max was liberated by the 761st Tank Battalion, a segregated unit of African American soldiers who had themselves experienced violent racist oppression at home. Some were only a couple of generations removed from slavery. (Twenty years ago, Max was reunited with

---

[*] "Dr. Tadeusz Orzeszko," on Polin: The History of the Polish Jews website, http://www.sprawiedliwi.org.pl/en/cms/your-stories/1077/.

[**] Ibid.

253

one of his liberators, Sergeant Johnnie Stevens, at a documentary screening in Toronto. Stevens was the grandson of slaves and the first African American bus driver in Middlesex County, New Jersey.* He remained in close contact with Max until his death in 2007.) Yet liberation was only one step in Max's long journey to a new life of stability in Canada—a journey that included a difficult recovery from pleurisy, the loss of his family home, and a six-month period of imprisonment in Communist Prague for forging false identification documents.

After decades of working as a committed and inspiring Holocaust speaker, Max wrote this memoir as a gift to his readers and a guarantee that his memories will endure for future generations. Despite several false starts and the nightmares that invaded his sleep when deep memories resurfaced, Max was determined to commit his story to paper—an act that speaks to his persistence and fortitude. Like many Holocaust survivors, he lived in part because of luck and circumstance, in part because of his relationships with people who afforded him lifesaving advice or a kind gesture, and in part because of his own personal strength, which allowed him to get through one impossible day after another. Working so closely with Max in the editing of this memoir is one of the highlights of my scholarly career, and I cherish the friendship we have developed over the last five years. His story is now yours.

—Amanda Grzyb, PhD

---

* "Obituary: Johnnie Stevens," *Star-Ledger* (Newark, NJ), July 16, 2007.

Acknowledgments

Of approximately sixty members of my extended family, only three of us survived: me; my maternal first cousin, Lily Friedman Kalish; and my paternal first cousin, Chaim (Tibor) Lazarovits. After the war, Lily immigrated to the United States and married an American veteran. She was the spitting image of my mother, and once I settled in Canada, we spoke on the phone biweekly. Chaim immigrated to Israel in 1947 and married an Israeli woman; I saw him annually in the last fifteen years of his life. Lily passed away on July 23, 2014, at the age of eighty-nine, and Chaim passed away on July 31, 2015, at the age of eighty-five. They were the only remnant of my first family, and the only people with whom I could reminisce about our previous life and our beloved family members—I am grateful for the bond that we shared after the Holocaust. Their deaths hit me hard and I feel the loss every day.

I would like to acknowledge all the people who assisted me in my recovery period after my initial return to Czechoslovakia as a survivor of the Nazi concentration camps. Ily Klinka, our family friend and neighbour, saw my distress and provided swift motherly actions, which led me to the St. Elizabeth Hospital in Košice. The dedicated nuns at St. Elizabeth pulled me through several difficult weeks of treatment for pleurisy. Joseph and Malvinka Gottlieb took me into their home without hesitation and gave me sustenance, and they, together with six others—their three daughters, Ilonka, Clari, and Shari; their son, Itzhak; their cousin Ruty; and their friend Magda—all contributed to a welcoming atmosphere and created a "home" for me. Malvinka's wonderful meals reminded me of my mother's and grandmother's preparations, and enabled me to put on weight and regain vitality.

As I continued along in my journey to health, I was assisted by the American Jewish Joint Distribution Committee, which supported a school for Jewish studies and vocational services in Marienbad, Czechoslovakia. The three years I spent there renewed my spirit, both physically and mentally. As the three years were coming to an end, Rabbi Abraham Price of Toronto was instrumental in securing my visa to come to Canada.

I want to acknowledge the support of the Holocaust Education Centre (under the auspices of the Jewish Federation of Toronto), which gave me the opportunity to speak to students from public schools, high schools, and universities, as well as adult groups. Likewise, I want to recognize the March of the Living Canada, under the direction of Eli Rubenstein and Michael Soberman. They demonstrate exceptional leadership and dedication, and provide an important service to the community. I acknowledge, too, all the friends, professors, students, and teachers who have provided a constant platform for me to expound on the lessons of the Shoah. I am hopeful the information I have offered will make a difference for them in the future, for the betterment of humankind.

My granddaughter Tziporah Sarah with my great-grandchildren: Yehudit (right), Elisheva (left), and Michael Aharon.

I am very thankful to the Friends of Simon Wiesenthal Center, under the direction of Avi Benlolo and his support staff, for giving me the opportunity to speak as a survivor educator in many of their educational programs. The Wiesenthal Center does important outreach work in the public sphere to educate and inform about the Holocaust and genocide. It was on one of their annual "Compassion to Action" missions to Poland that I met Jim Gifford, the editorial director for non-fiction at HarperCollins, who has been so supportive of my memoir project. I am grateful for Jim's editorial advice, his kindness, and his friendship. I am also indebted to my talented copyeditor, Janice Weaver, who went over the manuscript with such care and professionalism, and to my wonderful production editor, Maria Golikova, who helped keep the project on track. Professor Robert Jan van Pelt was kind enough to meet with me in Oświęcim in Summer 2015, and he helped me obtain releases for historical photographs of Auschwitz.

It seems to me that the stars were aligned in March 2010 when I first met Professor Amanda Grzyb, from the Faculty of Information and Media Studies at the University of Western Ontario, on the Simon Wiesenthal Center's inaugural mission to Poland. Through our common interest in Holocaust education, the seeds of our relationship were sown, and she played a vital role in the writing of this book. When I met Amanda, I had been speaking as a survivor educator for many years, but it was difficult for me to put my experiences down on paper. Amanda understood my frustrations and graciously offered her editorial assistance to help me overcome the obstacles that were preventing me from writing. With her help, I found my voice and my method of self-expression, and everything seemed to flow naturally from that point. Her research assistants, Amaal Mohamed Bhaloo, Kaitlyn Bida, and Jennifer Schmidt, assisted us both by transcribing our interviews. Amanda is a generous, thoughtful, and caring person, who has dedicated herself to educating others about the Holocaust, the Rwandan genocide, and other social injustices. I am proud to have her as a friend. I'm very grateful that she invested her valuable time in reading and editing my manuscript. She gave me the confidence to continue in an organized fashion, with a clear goal in mind. With her encouragement, I delved deep into the past and was able to bring long-forgotten, terrifying experiences to the forefront of my memory.

Our granddaughter Julie.

Finally, I want to express my deepest appreciation to my family. My in-laws, Rose and Sam Cosman, listened to my story and helped me along my journey. They became my second set of parents, and all their family members—their sons, Malcolm and Alvin, and their uncles, aunts, cousins, and sisters-in-law—accepted me in every respect. I owe an eternal gratitude to my beloved wife, Ivy, and my sons, Ed (who was a sounding board throughout this entire process) and Larry (who designed the maps in this book), for their love, support, and encouragement. They make my ship sail smoothly and are the stabilizers in my life. They are always there for me, and I can always count on their steadfastness. I'm fortunate to have two granddaughters, Amy Tzipporah Sarah and Julie Mina Leah, who have brought me great joy. And now a fourth generation is coming along, with three great-grandchildren so far: Yehudit, Elisheva, and Michael Aharon.

I send this book to publication with a feeling of great accomplishment. It was difficult to complete, but I'm relieved that my story can be shared with my family and others, who I hope will gain insight from it. Thank you for reading my words.

Appendix

Additional Documents

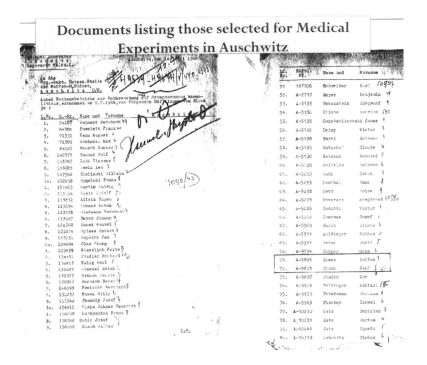

Documents listing those selected for Medical
Experiments in Auschwitz

In 1995 I discovered that my father and uncle were victims of Nazi medical experiments. Dr. Carson Phillips of the Neuberger Holocaust Centre in Toronto found documents showing their names on a July 1944 selection list in the Auschwitz archives.

Documents listing those selected for Medical Experiments in Auschwitz

The SS-Doctor (sth. like "SS-Locationdoctor, location means the camp/mil. Base)
Auschwitz
Campdoctor KL.Au.I (Concentrationcamp Auschwitz I)

Auschwitz, July 10th, 1944

To
Hygienic/bacterial examination center
Of the Waffen-SS, Southeast,
Auschwitz O/S (maybe "oberschlesien" / upper silesia)

Enclosed faucal smear tests for examination for "Streptococcus haemoliticus", taken on 9th of July 1944, from following prisoners of Block 5a:

Consecutive Number	Number of Prisoner	Name and forename	Result
71	A-9891	Eisen Zoltan	
72	A-9893	Eisen Jeno	

This and the following letter demostrate the dispassionate and mechanical approach of the engineers and SS officials involved in the logistics of mass murder.

Translation:

[Top left: Rubber stamp of the Topf management secretariat, dated 6th December 1941, with the initials of the directors: *LT* for Ludwig Topf and *ET* for Ernst-Wolfgang Topf, and the inscription *for reply* and *replied on*]

Erfurt, 6th December 1941

To Messrs
 Ludwig and Ernst Wolfgang Topf

       Inside the house

Dear Messrs Topf,

As you know, I designed both the 3 muffle and 8 muffle cremation furnaces, and this using mainly my free time—at home. These furnace constructions pioneer the way for the future and I venture to hope that you will grant me a bonus for the work involved.

     Heil Hitler!
     Kurt Prüfer

      On the order of LT/ET,
      150 RM paid 24/12/41
      [Initials]

(Braun), agreed
? must discuss
   T

Erfurt, den 15. November 1942

Herren
Ed. L. Topf!
im Hause.

Sehr geehrte Herren Topf!

Nach der Absprache mit Ihnen die Ende vorigen Jahres stattfand, haben Sie mir für die Neukonstruktion der Dreimuffel-Einäscherungsöfen, eine Entschädigung zugesagt.
Diese sollte gezahlt werden, sobald das einwandfreie Ergebnis für die Arbeitsweise der Öfen vorlag.
Vor 12 bzw. 6 Wochen sind die beiden oberirdischen
Topf-Dreimuffel-Einäscherungsöfen
im Krematorium Buchenwald in Betrieb gekommen.
Der erste Ofen hat bereits eine große Anzahl Einäscherungen hinter sich, die Arbeitsweise des Ofens und demzufolge die Neukonstruktion hat sich bewährt u. ist einwandfrei.
Die Öfen leisten so mehr, als von mir überhaupt vorgesehen war.
Es sind bis jetzt 8 Stk. Dreimuffel-Einäscherungsöfen fertiggestellt bzw. im Bau. Weitere 6 Stk. sind in Arbeit.
Deshalb bitte ich Sie, die mir versprochene Entschädigung baldigst anweisen zu wollen.

Stets gern zu Ihren Diensten
Ihr ergebener
Kurt Prüfer
Buchleben.
Neue Göringstr. 2

Translation:

[Manuscript] SS Second Lieutenant (Specialist) Kirschnick!

Copy

29th January, 1943

Correspondence register no 22250/43/Bi/L
Subject: Krematorium II. State of construction
Reference: SS-WVHA telegram 2648 of 28/1/43
Enclosure: 1 Inspection Report

Head of Amstgruppen C
SS Lieutenant-General and Waffen SS Major-General
Dr Ing (Engineer) Kammler

Berlin Lichterfelde West
Unter den Eichen 126-135

Krematorium II has been completed but for minor details, thanks to employing all available forces, despite enormous difficulties and freezing weather, using day and night shifts. The furnaces have been lit in the presence of Herr Chief Engineer Prüfer of the firm responsible for their construction, Topf & Sons of Erfurt and they function perfectly. Because of the frost, it has not yet been possible to remove the formwork from the ceiling of the corpse cellar. This is of no consequence, however, as the gassing cellar can be used to this end [i.e. a morgue].

Because the wagons are blocked, Messrs Topf & Sons have not been able to deliver on time the ventilation and air extraction installations as required by the Bauleitung. These will be fitted as soon as they arrive, so that it is probable that the installation will be entirely ready for service on the 20th February 1943.

Please find enclosed a report by the inspecting engineer of Topf & Sons, Erfurt.

Head of the Auschwitz Waffen SS and Police
Central Construction Management

[Signed] Bischoff
SS Captain

Distribution:
1 SS Second Lieutenants Janisch and Kirschneck
1 Registration

For Archives

[Signed] Pollok
SS Second Lieutenant (S)

Postscript

"May G-d bless you and safeguard you. May He be gracious unto you. May He turn His countenance to you and give you peace."

These were the words Max's father, standing behind the wires, shared with his son before their parting. Alas, he was fully aware of the fate which so soon awaited him, having been selected for death in the Auschwitz camp. How strong must a man be to say farewell to the last living member of his family, his beloved son, with the words of blessing he had repeated every Saturday to his children in his own quiet home, over a bountiful table, in the company of his wife and his parents—his happy family.

A family acquaintance, a forester, had warned them about the Nazis rounding up Hungarian Jews, but they were unable to escape before they were arrested. It was Passover Sabbath. Religious Jews, in their traditional attire, with their traditional way of life and traditional prayers, were the most exposed to danger during this time. It was easier for assimilated Jews to dress up, to find shelter, to hide, if they happened to meet moral people along the way.

Still, standing behind the wires, Max's father added the following, which has accompanied Max throughout his entire life: "If you survive, you must tell the world what happened here. Now go."

These were the words so often spoken by Auschwitz inmates who knew or felt that they would not survive. With these words, they shouldered their entire fate and the history of their agony upon their fellow inmates, family, and friends. With these words, they wanted to express the hope that someone—be it even a single person—would survive to testify to the tragic fate of the innocent victims at Germany's largest concentration and death camp. *Non omnis moriar.* (I shall not wholly die.)

Right after the war, suddenly alone in his now-hostile homeland, Max was for a long time unable to talk about what had happened to his relatives, his siblings, and his parents. "At that time, I could not yet fully comprehend the magnitude of the destruction of Jewish culture and people in Continental Europe, nor could I articulate the depth of my trauma or put my losses into words."

Is it really the case that after so many years have passed, it is easier to find the right words to script the drama written in the blood of innocent victims? Could such great cruelty make any sense after all this time has gone by? Do all those people—like the survivors, from whom the SS men and their collaborators stole not only childhood but also the peace of old age—go away, as if in a mist, whilst their senseless suffering becomes a well-polished literary subject?

Certainly not. And that is why this book was conceived. Firstly, to fulfil Max's father's will—his last, sacred words. Secondly, as a testimony to share with the world. And thirdly, so that people can truly take to heart the facts presented to them from no more than a few decades ago, written as young Max saw and experienced them.

In a sense, *By Chance Alone* is not the story of an individual life. It is the story of the millions whose stories could not be written. Together with the numerous accounts from other survivors, this book adds another perspective to the picture in its entirety. But it is only a picture, of course.

Max survived transport, selection, the hardships of slave labour, the death of his entire family, evacuation, transfers to other camps, liberation, isolation, Communist prison, and his escape to the West. He survived because more than once on his way he met people who wanted to help: the Polish surgeon, Dr. Tadeusz Orzeszko, and other doctors in attendance in Block 21; the Soviet POW, Misha, from the Melk camp; Ily, the woman who recognized his grave medical condition, and the good-natured secretary at the Canadian Embassy in Salzburg.

These were the people who made Max's father's words of hope, "*May G-d bless you and safeguard you,*" come true. And this book, written so many years afterward fulfils his father's final wish: "Tell the world what happened here."

—Piotr M. A. Cywiński
Director, Auschwitz-Birkenau Museum and Memorial

A Note on the Author

I n the early 2000s, I recall being with Max at Queen's University for a weekend conference, training the educators and chaperones who would be travelling with us to Poland for the March of the Living.

As we were milling about the reception area, a group of Queen's students passed by. They noticed one of our staff carrying a Sefer Torah (the Scroll of the Law), the ancient Five Books of Moses handwritten on parchment, which Jewish people have read from publicly for thousands of years.

Observing the looks of curiosity on the students' faces, Max explained that during the Holocaust, the Nazis burned thousands of sacred Jewish works, just like this Torah. He also reminded the students of the quote from Heinrich Heine: "Where they burn books, they will in the end also burn people." The students were mesmerized during Max's impromptu speech and only reluctantly tore themselves away to return to their school activities.

It was then that I realized Max was a born teacher who had both the desire and the ability to share the lessons of the

Holocaust with highly diverse audiences in the clearest, most accessible manner. When Max speaks, I can see how difficult it is for him, how he sees each and every member of his martyred family before his eyes. Nonetheless, for the past twenty-five years, Max has criss-crossed this country and travelled abroad to share his story hundreds of times. Such is his unwavering commitment to Holocaust education.

In his early life, Max suffered more than anyone can imagine, seeing endless cruelty, the abandonment of all human morality, and the loss of his entire family. And yet he went on to build a new life for himself. He came to Canada, started a business, got married—he had children, grandchildren, and even great-grandchildren.

Despite the horrendous brutality he underwent during the Holocaust, when Max tells his story, he always expresses gratitude for the people who helped him on the way. After all the bitter experiences and tragic events of his early life, Max reminds us to be grateful for the goodness life presents, and that one can always begin anew.

And if Max can do that, considering all that he has gone through, is that not a lesson for all of us, no matter what hardships we have experienced?

Max is one of my personal heroes, and after reading his exceptional story not only of tremendous loss, but also of courage and gratitude, I am almost certain you will regard him a hero as well.

—Eli Rubenstein
National Director, March of the Living Canada
Director of Education, March of the Living International